Palgrave Pivots in Sports Economics

This mid-length monograph series invites contributions between 25,000–50,000 words in length, and considers the economic analysis of sports from all aspects, including but not limited to: the demand for sports, broadcasting and media, sport and health, mega-events, sports accounting, finance, betting and gambling, sponsorship, regional development, governance, competitive balance, revenue sharing, player unions, pricing and ticketing, regulation and anti-trust, and, globalization. Sports Economics is a rapidly growing field and this series provides an exciting new publication outlet enabling authors to generate reach and impact.

More information about this series at
http://www.palgrave.com/gp/series/15189

Yvan J. Kelly · David Berri ·
Victor A. Matheson

The Economics of the Super Bowl

Players, Performers, and Cities

palgrave
macmillan

Yvan J. Kelly
Flagler College
St. Augustine, FL, USA

Victor A. Matheson
Department of Economics and Accounting
College of the Holy Cross
Worcester, MA, USA

David Berri
Department of Economics and Finance
Southern Utah University
Cedar City, UT, USA

ISSN 2662-6438 ISSN 2662-6446 (electronic)
Palgrave Pivots in Sports Economics
ISBN 978-3-030-46369-4 ISBN 978-3-030-46370-0 (eBook)
https://doi.org/10.1007/978-3-030-46370-0

This Palgrave Macmillan imprint is published by the registered company Springer Nature Switzerland AG
The registered company address is: Gewerbestrasse 11, 6330 Cham, Switzerland

To Kris and Allie, and to the teams I coached and scouted for who were Knights, Warriors, Tigers, Saints, Lakers, Sonics, Nuggets and Rockets. Thousands of miles and thousands of games, but never a first down.

—Yvan J. Kelly.

This book is dedicated to my wife Lynn and my daughters Allyson and Jessica. I would have also loved to mention how much the Detroit Lions—who have been my team since the 1970s—have inspired my interest in the Super Bowl. But since the Lions have only won a single playoff game in my entire lifetime, it would be disingenuous for me to do so!!!

—David Berri

This book is dedicated to Jolie, Lara, and Aly for always making life worth living. I would also like to thank my original hometown team, the Denver Broncos, for first inspiring my interest in the Super Bowl by managing to lose their first four trips to the big game during my formative years as a sports fan by a combined score of 163-50. What a great preparation to enter the "dismal science."

—Victor A. Matheson

Acknowledgments

The authors wish to thank all those who assisted with this project. Hannah Whipple, a Research Assistant at Flagler College, worked on this project and did an admiral job of tracking down sources and accumulating data. Thanks also to Carrie Grant and Kurt Sebastian from the math department at Flagler who provided keen insights into the testing of the data. A good amount of the data used in this book is proprietary and not generally available to the public. Despite that, there are many who provided us this information and who wish to remain anonymous. They will go unnamed here, but you know who you are and you know this book could not have been written without you. A great thanks goes to Garen Vande Beek, former Senior Executive Vice President at CBS, who helped provide insights about the broadcast history of the Super Bowl as well as the production of the game.

Contents

Abbreviations

AAFC	All-American Football Conference
ABC	American Broadcasting Company
AFC	American Football Conference
AFL	American Football League
APFA	American Professional Football Association
CBS	Columbia Broadcasting System
CD	Compact Disc
EMS	Emergency Medical Services
ESPN	Entertainment and Sports Programming Network
FOX	Fox Broadcasting Company
IMPLAN	Impact Analysis for Planning
MRP	Marginal Revenue Product
NBA	National Basketball Association
NBC	National Broadcasting Company
NFC	National Football Conference
NFL	National Football League
PGA	Professional Golfers Association
RIMS II	Regional Input–Output Multiplier System
SAG-AFTRA	Screen Actors Guild-American Federation of Television and Radio Artists
SMRI	Sports Management Research Institute
UCR	Uniform Crime Reports
UEFA	Union of European Football Associations

List of Figures

List of Tables

CHAPTER 1

Introduction

Abstract The 1966 merger of the NFL and the AFL led to the playing of a championship game, initially titled the NFL–AFL World Championship. That bulky name was soon dropped and the game is now commonly referred to as the Super Bowl. The game has grown in societal importance and become part of the cultural fabric of the United States. This chapter provides an overview of the economics of the three major components of the game that are covered in this book: the football players, the cities that host the games, and the halftime artists.

Keywords Player valuation · Economic impact · Song consumption valuation

Nothing on the US sports scene compares to the Super Bowl. The championship game of the National Football League (NFL) is a social phenomenon which dominates sports coverage for the two weeks leading up to the game, is annually the most watched sporting event in the country, and is the justification for social gatherings and parties throughout the land. Over the years, the game has taken on a global interest and is broadcast internationally.

Fans from across the country who are able to get tickets to the game flock to the host cities. There, they stay several days in hotels, eat in the restaurants, enjoy local entertainment, and enjoy the excitement and

Y. J. Kelly et al., *The Economics of the Super Bowl*, Palgrave Pivots in Sports Economics, https://doi.org/10.1007/978-3-030-46370-0_1

anticipation of the big game. Corporations host private and exclusive parties rewarding their most accomplished employees and best customers. There is a lot of money spent in the host city as a result of the presence of the Super Bowl. But what exactly are the benefits from hosting the game? Are the benefits as large as popularly reported?

For NFL players, reaching the championship game is the pinnacle of their professional playing career. Being able to play in the Super Bowl is a dream most players have had since they began playing the game as a child. To be a champion might mean more to the players than the bonus money they receive for the victory. Perhaps there is a financial incentive to reach the title game and to be successful once there. Specifically, does winning a Super Bowl impact future pay? And does winning a Super Bowl have any impact on the future revenues of the championship team?

As part of the celebration of the game, the NFL puts on an elaborate and expensive halftime show featuring some of the top musical stars of the day as well as legacy stars who have had long and very successful careers. It is surprising to some to learn that the featured artists are compensated with only the union's minimum pay scale. Surely, there must be some financial benefit to the artists for having practically volunteered their time to be the halftime performer. Where do the musical artists see the payoff? Is it in the consumption of their music following the game? Is it in future concert revenues? Are there other revenue sources from which they benefit from having been the halftime act? And what about the cheerleaders who typically perform at each game? What are they paid to perform on the NFL's biggest stage?

This book is designed to explore these three areas: players, cities, and performers. Chapter 2 of this book will begin with a brief history of the NFL and its mergers with rival leagues over the years. The most important merger for the NFL was that with the American Football League (AFL) in 1966. This agreement for a merger led to an interleague championship game, the NFL—AFL World Championship Game. That game was renamed the Super Bowl and is marked by using Roman numerals rather than the year when the games are played.

The remaining chapters will then examine the benefits for each of these groups who participate in the Super Bowl: the cities who host the game, the players, and the performers. Building upon previous research in the labor economics and player valuation in football, the benefits to the players for participating in the game will be explored.

Chapter 3 will explore the economic impact for cities that host the Super Bowl. A historical background of cities who have hosted the game will be presented. The cities selected to host the Super Bowl, host the game expecting to receive an economic benefit. There are ex ante estimates that have been made about just how much a city will benefit from hosting all those fans arriving for the game. Problems occur within these ex ante economic impact studies that tend to overstate the benefits the city will receive. The sources of the problems and the reasons for the overstatement of benefits will be explored. An examination of the costs of hosting the game will also be presented. Ex post economic impact studies will be used to compare the differences between what cities hoped to have happened as a result of hosting the game with what actually happened as a result. There are also non-monetary benefits for the host city which are explored.

Chapter 4 explores the team and players in the game. This chapter begins with a discussion of how winning the Super Bowl impacts team revenues. It will then move on to a discussion of the most important player on the field. The quarterback—or the "face of the franchise"—is often given credit when his team wins. We will also see, there is some evidence that the winning quarterback sees his future pay increase from winning this game. What may be surprising is the winning quarterback isn't often the "best" quarterback.

Chapter 5 will explore the benefits to the other performers (i.e., not the teams!) at the Super Bowl. We will begin with a discussion of halftime performers. That discussion will begin with the history of the halftime show and the mostly forgotten reason this spectacle expanded in the early 1990s. The benefits for halftime artists will be examined and estimates will be made for the value of the song consumption of their music prior to and following the game. The estimates point to a very large bump for the artists in the consumption of their music through the means of downloads, audio streaming, and video streaming. Musical artists also generate substantial revenues from concerts. The impact that being the halftime performer at the Super Bowl has on future concert revenues will be examined. By measuring the average gross concert revenues for artists the year prior to and the year following their Super Bowl appearance, an analysis is made concerning whether a benefit is present from being the featured artist at the game. This area of study is unique to the sports economics literature.

The halftime performers are not the only non-players to put on a show at the Super Bowl. Cheerleaders have been part of this game for decades. The most famous of these are the Dallas Cowboys Cheerleaders. Although these cheerleaders became quite famous in the 1970s, their pay did not match their notoriety. In fact, the Dallas Cowboys Cheerleaders weren't even paid when they performed at the 1978 Super Bowl. A lack of pay remains an issue for the NFL's cheerleaders. As we will argue, the same reason halftime performers benefit so much from appearing at these games is also why cheerleaders are paid so little.

Chapter 6 will summarize the findings and draw conclusions. This book is purposely limited in its scope and intentionally focuses on the three major participants in the game: the cities, the players, and the performers. It is the hope of the authors that future researchers will be interested enough in these topics to further explore these areas and further develop and refine our theories. For the casual fan of the professional football, the hope is that this book will provide a deeper understanding of the makeup of the game as well as giving some behind the scenes insights.

CHAPTER 2

The Origins of the NFL and the Super Bowl

Abstract Professional football grew from the popularity of the collegiate game. The NFL began as a small, regional league and grew to become the preeminent sport in the United States. As it grew in size and financial stability, the NFL faced several challenges from rival leagues. In 1966, the NFL agreed to slowly merge with the AFL and to establish a World Championship game. That championship game, now known as the Super Bowl, is the most watched televised event in the country. The game has grown to become a massive event and very big business.

Keywords NFL History · NFL–AFL merger · Super Bowl growth

From its humble and financially tenuous beginnings in 1920, the National Football League has grown to become the premier spectator sport of the United States (Crepeau 2014). Likewise, its championship game, the Super Bowl, has become North America's most watched sporting event (Stewart 2002). The NFL's growth in popularity is demonstrated by the size of its weekly television viewership and the national interest generated in the championship game. This chapter will examine the history of the NFL, its rise in popularity, and the emergence of the Super Bowl as both a financial juggernaut and cultural icon of American society. Later chapters

Y. J. Kelly et al., *The Economics of the Super Bowl*, Palgrave Pivots in Sports Economics, https://doi.org/10.1007/978-3-030-46370-0_2

will examine the economic impact that participating in the game brings to players, halftime performers, and the cities which host the game.

During its growth, the popularity of the NFL surpassed that of baseball, which had formerly captivated the interest of Americans and which was once known as America's pastime (Surdam 2013). The NFL was founded at a time when collegiate football was widely popular but baseball was the leading professional sport. In its infancy, the league was hardly even considered a substitute good for the college game, and it undoubtedly lagged behind both horse racing and boxing in terms of popularity among the masses. The likelihood that the NFL would survive, much less rise in prominence was improbable. Its financing was dubious, and its chances for survival seemed scant (MacCambridge 2005). In fact, between 1920 and 1935, over 50 teams played at least one season in the NFL, 43 of which had folded or relocated by the end of that era (Leeds et al. 2018). But from those modest beginnings, the league survived the Depression and World War II before exploding in popularity after the war.

From a sociological perspective, it is difficult to pinpoint why the NFL grew in popularity. In the 1920s and 1930s, fans, especially males, seemed to be attracted to the brute force of the professional game (Crepeau 2014). The contact between players was harder, and the players were faster, larger, and in general, meaner than college players. It appears that the violence of the game was a major attraction in the early years of professional football. Following World War II, the game was seen as a "training and moral vehicle for the young men of the nation" (Crepeau 2014, p. 32). In the 1950s and 1960s, rivalries both between teams and between leagues had developed which helped fuel the popularity of professional football (MacCambridge 2005).

The league especially enjoyed a tremendous growth in popularity with the increase of the number of televisions in homes during the 1960s (Crepeau 2014). The dawn of television brought the game into the homes of Americans looking for Sunday afternoon entertainment. This served to further increase the number of NFL fans, developing a demand for the product that stretched beyond the cities where the games were played and creating loyal fans located across the country (Surdam 2013). Fan interest in the championship game continued to grow along with the increasing popularity of the NFL. Indeed, the size and scope of the Super Bowl has now become an important part of the fabric of American society each February. It is a singular event unmatched by any other in American sport.

The Super Bowl has become a reflection of modern American society. The host cities witness tens of thousands of fans descending on them for the big game, corporations host lavish parties during Super Bowl week, hotels fill up with fans paying extraordinarily high room rates, restaurants see record business, local airports are filled with private jets bringing in wealthy attendees of the game, and advertisers create new and creative television ads for the broadcast. The host cities themselves spend large sums on infrastructure improvements such as roadways, beautification projects, and increased security, all in preparation for the large influx of sports tourists. Even if we view the word "excess" as a relative term, the Super Bowl must be acknowledged for its extravagance. It operates on a staggering scale when the total amount of spending done by visitors, advertisers, and on production costs is considered (Crepeau 2014). The result of this extravagance is that the Super Bowl is the most watched event on American television (Stewart 2002). There simply is nothing else like it on the US sports scene or indeed anywhere else in American popular culture.

Thorstein Veblen, author of The Theory of the Leisure Class, died long before the Super Bowl era but we can speculate that he would have enjoyed applying his concepts of conspicuous consumption and conspicuous waste to what he would have observed in the events surrounding the game. The millions of fans who do not travel to the game but who host parties in their homes and who cheer for the teams on the field demonstrate the type of vicarious conspicuous leisure of which Veblen wrote (Veblen 2009). In short, the NFL and the Super Bowl have permeated the fabric of American culture. The journey to reach this place in society has been nothing short of remarkable.

A Brief History of the NFL

The NFL was not the first football league in the United States nor was it even the first professional league. Football's origins in the United States can be traced back as far as November 6, 1869, when Rutgers and the College of New Jersey (now more regally known as Princeton) played the first college football game. The match, however, was played with rules more resembling today's soccer than American football, and it wasn't until 1874 when Harvard first played Tufts using rules that could reasonably be described as a forerunner of modern American football. The college game far exceeded the professional version in popularity for the first half century of the sport, but paid athletes playing outside the confines of academia began to arise in the 1890s. William "Pudge" Heffelfinger became the first professional football player, or at least the first pro known to history, when he accepted $500 to play a game for the Allegheny Athletic Association in Pittsburgh on November 12, 1892 (Pro Football Hall of Fame 2020). Semi-professional football leagues, or more accurately, loose associations of various teams, popped up in numerous states across the East and Midwest including Illinois, New York, Pennsylvania, and most importantly for the development of the modern NFL, in Ohio. The so-called Ohio League organized a championship for its members each year between 1902 and 1919. While a far cry from the modern NFL, the league did attract crowds numbering in the thousands, and it had its very own scandal in 1906 when it is alleged that the Canton Bulldogs and Massillon Tigers conspired to fix a series of games (Braunwart and Carroll 1984). Thus, the Ohio League served as a forerunner to both the NFL itself and to misdeeds in the NFL such as the New England Patriots' infamous "Inflategate."

In 1920, four of the Ohio League's members, Canton, Cleveland, Dayton, and Akron, formed the American Professional Football Association (APFA) in an attempt to both formalize the league and expand the footprint of the league beyond the state of Ohio (Crepeau 2014). Within two months the league had expanded, first to seven and then to 15 teams. The intention of the league was to build on the intense interest in high school and collegiate football following World War I. The APFA was financially weak after the first year of play and its future existence was in jeopardy. The league chose to expand, in hopes that having more teams would also allow more teams to survive. The league was playing a numbers game; if more franchises were started, even though many would fail, the probability of another season of play would increase. For the 1921 season, the Association grew to 21 teams but only 13 survived the year.

In 1922, the Association was renamed the National Football League and began play with 18 teams (MacCambridge 2005). At the time, the NFL consisted of a combination of teams which were permanently located in cities and others that were barnstorming teams. A barnstorming team is one that travels from town to town playing local teams and has no home stadium or home games. As an example, the early NFL team the Duluth Eskimos played no home games (Crepeau 2014).

Whether the teams were barnstorming or not, many played games against local opponents that were not members of the NFL. Some of the teams also played more games in a season than others. As a result, because of the varying quantity and quality of opponents, it was very difficult for the NFL to determine who was the league champion each year. A league committee would convene at the end of the season and vote to crown the NFL champion (Stewart 2002). This method of selecting the league champion was similar to what was being used at the time to determine the national champion in collegiate football. In collegiate football, voting was done and a national champion was selected prior to the colleges playing postseason bowl games (MacCambridge 2005).[1]

The first NFL championship game wasn't played until the 12th season of the league's existence. Even then, this first attempt at a championship game in 1932 between the Chicago Bears and the Portsmouth Spartans was highly unusual. The two teams had tied for the best regular season record and an additional game was scheduled between the two teams to determine the champion. The game was to be played in Chicago, but due to bad weather the game was moved from an outdoor football stadium to an indoor basketball arena. Dirt was brought into the arena to create a field of play, but because of the dimensions of the arena, the field was shortened and narrowed from those used during the regular season games (Crepeau 2014). The following year, 1933, the first championship game was played in earnest with the Chicago Bears beating the New York Giants (NFL History 2020).

Despite not having a true postseason championship game in its early years, fan interest in professional football began to take hold during the mid-1920s. In 1925 the highly popular player Red Grange joined the league bringing with him notoriety, fans, and profits (Crepeau 2014). Entrepreneurs recognizing an opportunity for profits formed a rival league, the American Football League (AFL). This name would prove to be popular through the years as several rival leagues were to later form and take that same name.

This original AFL consisted of seven regular teams and two barnstorming teams that only played road games. The NFL responded to the new league by expanding its own number of franchises. As economic theory would predict, the increased competition for players between the

[1] In college football, while the election process was eventually moved to after the bowl games, the practice of voting on a national champion stayed in place until the formation of the Bowl Coalition in 1992.

two leagues began to increase player salaries. That, added to the distribution of the population of the fan base, placed the AFL teams under a great financial strain. Only four AFL teams survived its first season. By the 1927 season, the AFL had merged with the NFL on the NFL's terms. As an example, the New York Yankees of the AFL were only allowed to play four home games and were forced to play 12 road games so as not to compete with the NFL's New York Giants team. Following the merger, the resulting NFL had 12 teams and also star players. It was no longer a barnstorming league (Crepeau 2014).

The years of the Great Depression and World War II were difficult for the NFL. The goal of the league was merely to survive. Most of the small market teams failed, with only Green Bay surviving (MacCambridge 2005). The league embraced having games broadcast on radio, which was a growing medium. The increased radio coverage, combined with newspaper coverage and movie newsreels helped boost the popularity of the league and also helped promote interest in star players. Wealthy men, either seeking the glory of owning a professional team or seeing potential profit opportunities at some point in the future, became owners of teams, bringing financial stability to the league as well as stabilizing the locations of the teams (Crepeau 2014). The NFL found itself becoming a viable major sports entity.

In 1935 and again in 1940, the NFL faced challenges as two rival leagues formed. Both leagues named themselves the American Football League. This time there was to be no merger. Both AFL attempts quickly failed and folded.

NFL play continued during World War II, but just as with the rest of the nation, it became a time of sacrifices and rationing. The league faced restrictions on travel from the Department of War Transportation. The NFL responded by cutting 27% from their travel spending (Crepeau 2014). Team rosters were cut from 33 players per team to 25 players (MacCambridge 2005). Several teams suspended operations, including the Los Angeles Rams, as they faced a difficulty with the draft and not having enough manpower to field teams. This difficulty was not with the NFL player draft but the US draft for military service. By May 1942, 36% of NFL players had been drafted for military service (MacCambridge 2005). During the 1943 and 1944 seasons, some teams temporarily combined into one. For example, the Pittsburgh Steelers and the Philadelphia Eagles combined to become the Steagles, sharing home games between the two cities (Football and America, 2020).

The NFL practiced acts of patriotism during the war years. It was during this time that the NFL began playing the national anthem prior to games. The league sold $4 million dollars of war bonds at games in the 1942 season, the equivalent of almost $66 million in 2020 dollars. The league also raised $680,000 for war relief charities that year (Crepeau 2014), the equivalent of over $11 million in 2020 dollars. By the end of the war, a total of 638 NFL players had fought in the war, with 19 being killed in action (MacCambridge 2005).

Following the War, teams were restored and rosters were expanded. Professional football was a sport positioned for an explosion of popularity. Famous sports writer John Lardner described football as being the game of the future (Crepeau 2014).

This environment lead to another challenge from a new rival league. In 1946, the All-American Football Conference (AAFC) formed. The AAFC drew fans during its first year as it spent heavily on players. This increase in demand for players resulted in increased player salaries, the Rams seeing their payroll increase by 32% (Crepeau 2014). The NFL had no interest in playing teams from this upstart league. They feared that doing so may signal the market that it considered the new league as being on the same level of play as the NFL (Surdam 2013). The second year of the AAFC was not as financially successful for them. Facing losses, it approached the NFL with an offer to merge. The two leagues merged in 1949 with the Browns, Colts, and 49ers all joining the NFL ranks.

The 1950s saw the NFL continue to solidify as a popular and financially stable league. Attendance grew throughout the decade (Crepeau 2014). Teams began to sign contracts selling local and regional T.V. rights. The different market sizes where the teams were located resulted in the broadcast revenues being uneven across the league. In 1953, the Los Angeles Rams broadcast contract brought in $100,000 for the team while the Green Bay Packers brought in only $5,000 (MacCambridge 2005).

Despite adding broadcast revenues for local teams, the NFL was at first concerned about the broadcasting of games on television. The league feared that having games shown on television would hurt gate revenues. This prisoner's dilemma seemed to be resolved in 1956 when CBS paid $1 million to the NFL for the rights to broadcast league games for that season (Crepeau 2014). This increase in revenue would more than offset any individual team decline in attendance. Television was now seen as a complimentary method of generating revenue and promoting the league.

However, any attempts by the NFL to negotiate a league-wide broadcasting rights would run afoul of the Federal Court's decision in United States v. National Football League (1953) limiting the league's ability to make television broadcasting decisions on behalf of its member teams. Thus, to be able to negotiate a league-wide broadcasting contract, the NFL needed and received a favorable piece of legislation. Congress passed the "sports bill" in 1959 giving the league some limited antitrust exemptions (Surdam 2013). In 1960, the NFL signed a $3.5 million-dollar exclusive national broadcasting contract with CBS (Surdam 2013). Prior to this, some teams had been on NBC or regional networks. In 1961, the owners gave new commissioner Pete Rozelle the ok to negotiate a $9.3 million-dollar two-year television deal.

Citing their previous decision in United States v. National Football League (1953) the courts said "no" to this new television agreement, ruling that it was an antitrust violation. Rozelle turned to a Congressman from Green Bay, John Byrnes, to have a new act passed that would permit negotiating a league-wide television contract and allowing the league to negotiate as a unit on behalf of the member teams. President John F. Kennedy, a man who had made games of touch football popular, signed the bill in October of 1961 (Surdam 2013). The following year, CBS agreed to pay the league $14 million per year for the rights to broadcast their games (Crepeau 2014).

As television took over American homes during the 1950s and 1960s, the NFL took over in popularity of broadcast sports. The NFL began to craft its image, changing rules to make the game more exciting and promoting the use of face masks and other safety equipment for its players. The now financially stable and well-established league was set to become the monopolist of professional football and was preparing to exploit all those advantages. But as is often the case in markets when there are no barriers to entry, when profits appear so do competitors.

The AFL–NFL Merger

The well-funded oil tycoon Lamar Hunt wanted to buy an NFL franchise in 1959 and move it to his home city of Dallas. When this proved unsuccessful, he asked the league to consider offering him an expansion franchise, but the NFL was hesitant to expand again so soon. The owners seemed to prefer to keep the supply of teams restricted, thus raising the value of each franchise. When his efforts to join the NFL failed, Hunt and fellow oil baron "Bud" Adams decided to back a new rival league, the cleverly named American Football League (AFL). Hotel magnate-Barron Hilton and other wealthy investors were also involved as financial supporters of this new league.

The NFL had no desire to face yet another rival league so soon. They offered franchises to Hunt and Adams if they would abandon their plans for the AFL. This time, Hunt was the one saying no. The NFL, which had underestimated the resolve of Hunt, began to see that the new rival league would become a formidable challenge (Surdam 2013).

The AFL announced its plans for team locations. Among the cities chosen for franchises were Dallas and Minneapolis. The NFL countered by rushing in, seeking to create new expansion franchises in those two markets. The AFL filed a $10 million-dollar antitrust suit against the NFL for doing this, but the suit failed (Surdam 2013). In their decision in AFL v. NFL (1960), court reasoned that the NFL was not duty-bound to make entry into the market easy for the AFL and that the country still had enough existing viable cities to allow the AFL to begin play. Expanding into markets that might be attractive to potential competitors was not considered predatory behavior on the part of the NFL. Following the decision, the owner of the Minneapolis franchise decided to change allegiances and jumped from starting an AFL team to forming an NFL team. The AFL, now shut out of the Minneapolis market, countered by locating a franchise in Oakland, California instead.

Besides having ownership with deep pockets, the AFL utilized a television revenue sharing plan that had first been proposed by Bill Veeck to Major League Baseballin 1952 (Crepeau 2014).The AFL's plan was to evenly share the proceeds from their national broadcast contract among the franchises (Surdam 2013). This was unlike the NFL's negotiated deals. The ABC television network, which had dropped their extensive coverage of boxing, was looking for sports programming. ABC offered the AFL $8.5 million over five years (Crepeau 2014). During the first year of the contract each team received $170,000, but by year five of the contract that amount grew to $225,000 per team (Crepeau 2014). This meant that some AFL teams had higher broadcast revenue than some NFL teams did, and the AFL had not even played a game yet! Having that television contract gave the AFL an advantage that the AAFC never had (Surdam 2013). It provided them with a mechanism to promote their league while also generating substantial revenues for its teams.

In the first year of AFL play, the NFL averaged 42,207 in attendance while the AFL averaged 16,351 per game (Crepeau 2014). The AFL attendance figures may not be paid attendance figures as that league gave away many tickets in promotional efforts. The NFL had higher television ratings than the AFL as well.

Ratings and attendance were not the only differences between the leagues. The style of play differed as well. The NFL featured more of a ball control ground game, while the AFL featured more passing and a more wide-open style of play. In some ways, the two playing styles reflected the cultural wars that the United States was experiencing during the 1960s (Felser 2008). The NFL displayed a conservative style of play while the AFL's was far more liberal. These terms could also be applied to the two leagues' approaches to black athletes. The NFL employed African American players from the very beginning, but by 1934 the league had become completely racially segregated. At least one owner, George Preston Marshall, "openly refused to allow. black athletes on his Boston Braves/Washington Redskins team, and reportedly pressured the rest of the league to follow suit.[2] The NFL did not have another black player until after World War II" (Remember the AFL 2020), and even then integration was forced upon the league as a condition of the Los Angeles Rams' lease with the L.A. Coliseum. Without an historical aversion to hiring black players, and with a willingness to look for talent at smaller colleges including historically black colleges traditionally overlooked by the NFL, the AFL integrated more rapidly than the NFL (Ross 1999). Whether or not either of these two factors led to stimulating fan interest in the game would be mere speculation, but it is a possibility.

By 1966 the average attendance had grown for the AFL to 34,291 per game. Television ratings for the league improved as well. These improvements followed the signing of big-name players into that league. Louisiana State University star Billy Cannon had been offered an NFL contract of $30,000 per year for three years along with a $10,000 signing bonus. He turned it down. The Houston Oilers of the AFL had offered him $110,000 per year (Crepeau 2014). As expected, the competition between the two leagues began to drive player salaries higher. In 1967, when the AFL spent $25 million in signing bonuses alone, the owners

[2] It remains a shocking surprise that the team with the league's most racist owner ended up with the what was, until 2020, the league's most racist mascot.

began to push for a merger with the NFL in an effort to contain costs (Crepeau 2014).

Peter Rozelle, who had been named the commissioner of the NFL in 1960 as a compromise candidate among the owners, had worked hard to establish himself as a strong leader for the league (Crepeau 2014). Because of the personalities involved in the leadership of the two leagues and the distrust between them, a merger would be a difficult accomplishment. The two leagues, though, did find some early ways to contain costs. The AFL and the NFL had a gentlemen's agreement not to poach players from each other's leagues. They would only compete for college players, but would leave the players currently on rosters alone. This agreement held until 1966 when the NFL New York Giants signed the kicker Ed Gogolak from the roster of the AFL Buffalo Bills. The fear was that the two leagues would start to compete for current players, thus driving up player costs even more. This is indeed what happened as the AFL Oakland Raiders signed quarterback Roman Gabriel from the NFL Los Angeles Rams. The AFL Houston Oilers then signed quarterback John Brodie from the San Francisco 49ers. As both leagues began to feel the financial pinch of these types of actions, both felt that the time for a merger had come.

Rozelle directed secret merger talks between the NFL and the AFL. An agreement was reached that would begin with a common draft between the two leagues to be held in 1966. Expansion teams would be added, all the existing AFL teams would be absorbed into the NFL, and the full integration between the two leagues would be completed by the 1970 season. It was also agreed that an interleague world championship game would be played starting at the end of the 1966 season (Felser 2008).

Part of the reason for this prolonged, gradual merger was that the two leagues each had television contracts that still had four years left on them. The goal was to continue individual league play over the lifetime of those contracts. When the separate contracts expired, a new unified NFL contract would be negotiated.

The merger of the two leagues was going to require either an approval from the Department of Justice or a new piece of Congressional legislation. The Department of Justice was not inclined to approve the merger on antitrust grounds and so NFL leadership approached members of Congress for help. With the merger facing possible antitrust violations, Congress would be needed to approve an exception to any antitrust activities the merger would present. Hale Boggs, a Congressman from

Louisiana was the pivotal person in this legislative process. Boggs had recently voted in favor of a civil rights bill. This vote cost him some popularity back in his Congressional district. To regain favor with his constituents, he promised to spearhead the merger legislation and push for it to be passed provided that the city of New Orleans would receive an expansion franchise NFL team. Once assured of that, Boggs attached the merger bill to another piece of needed legislation, thus ensuring that it would pass (Felser 2008). President Lyndon Johnson signed the bill into law without hesitation.

The final pieces of the merger included the league being split into two conferences, the National Football Conference (NFC) and the American Football Conference (AFC) with three divisions each. To balance the number of teams in each conference, the NFL franchises in Baltimore, Cleveland, and Pittsburg moved into the AFC, and were financially rewarded $3 million dollars each for doing so (MacCambridge 2005).

The Birth and Growth of the Super Bowl

The merger of the two leagues led to a world championship game to be played between the NFL and the AFL champions with the first game to be played in January of 1967. This makes the game the youngest of the major team sports championships in the United States (Stewart 2002). Finances aside, it was an opportunity for the AFL to prove that its level of play was on par with that of the NFL. It was a chance to prove themselves equal on the playing field (Felser 2008). In a short time, they were able to do just that.

Lamar Hunt was the first to call the championship game the Super Bowl (Crepeau 2014). The name indicated a higher level of play than college bowl games such as the Cotton Bowl, Rose Bowl, and Sugar Bowl. The name also cleverly played on the name of a popular toy at the time, the Super Ball, which had been introduced in 1966 (MacCambridge 2005). Hunt's nickname for the game stuck and it was first officially used by the NFL in the Fourth World Championship Game (Crepeau 2014).

Because the game was played in January of the year following the conclusion of the regular season, the dating of the championship became a question. If, say, a team played the 1968 season and made it to the championship game, the game would be played in 1969. Did that make the team the 1968 champions or the 1969 champions? The solution to the problem was to title the game with a Roman numeral. Doing so dropped any specific year or season question that may arise. Super Bowl V was the first to use Roman numerals when the title of World Championship Game was dropped. All previous World Championship games were retroactively renamed Super Bowl I to IV (Crepeau 2014).[3]

The first NFL–AFL World Championship game was shown on two television networks. This was because the two leagues had separate television contracts. CBS, who had broadcast NFL games that season, paid $1,000,000 to broadcast the game. NBC, who had broadcast AFL games, also paid $1,000,000 to be able to broadcast the game (Crepeau 2014). That year CBS charged advertiser $42,500 for a 30 second spot, while NBC charged its advertisers $35,000 for a 30 second spot. (Crepeau 2014).

That first game was played at the Los Angeles Memorial Coliseum. The Green Bay Packers from the NFL played the Kansas City Chiefs of the AFL. While there were 63,036 people in attendance, there were also about 30,000 empty seats (Crepeau 2014). Ticket prices for that game were $6, $10, and $12 (Felser 2008). Because of NFL blackout rules on televised games, and since the game was not a sellout, the game was not available for viewing in the Los Angeles area. Nationally though, the television ratings for the game were high.

The Packers won both Super Bowls I and II. Stewart (2002) speculates that if the NFL had won Super Bowl III as well, that the perceived lack of parity between the two leagues may have resulted in the merger being called off. The New York Jets of the AFL defeated the Baltimore Colts of the NFL in Super Bowl III and the AFL now had a claim that it was indeed equal to the NFL. Super Bowl IV saw the last game played by the AFL as the Kansas City Chiefs defeated the Minnesota Vikings. Ironically in 1971 at Super Bowl V, the first year after the fully completed merger, the Baltimore Colts won the game while representing the AFC.

As the popularity of the game increased, so did the production value of the game. In Super Bowl II, which was broadcast only by CBS, 12 cameras and one blimp were used. In 2020, FOX used 70 cameras, including robots (Kerschbaumer 2020). The scope of the game has increased as well. Cities hosting the games spend large amounts in preparation and in events surrounding the game. Corporations host exclusive parities and use private jets for their executives and guests. As a reflection

[3] Indeed, one sign of just how significant the game is in the United States is the fact that it almost single-handedly keeps the Roman numeral system alive in modern America.

of the people staying at home hosting Super Bowl viewing parties, sales of T.V.s increase the week prior to the game (Crepeau 2014). The popularity has increased worldwide as well and the game is now broadcast to 170 countries and 750 million people (Crepeau 2014).

Advertising during the game has become a spectator sport itself. Bleacher Report and Athlon Sports rank the best commercials shown each year during the game. Because the commercials are seen by such a large audience, the cost of advertising is high but so is the benefit. In 1984 Apple introduced its new computer, the MacIntosh, using a Super Bowl commercial and saw $4.6 million dollars' worth of computers sold within six hours of the broadcast (Crepeau 2014).[4] Hartmann and Klapper (2017) detail the correlation between viewership of the game and the effects of television advertising on sales following the game.

Currently, the broadcasting of the game is annually rotated between the three networks that broadcast NFL regular season games, FOX, NBC, and CBS. There can be exceptions to this. For example, in 2021 it is NBC's turn to show the game, but it will broadcast instead by CBS. The reason for this is that NBC has the rights to show the 2022 Winter Olympics and wants to have this complementary coverage by showing both in the same year. The NFL asked CBS if they would trade the 2022 Super Bowl for the 2021 game, to which CBS agreed. CBS, which rotates the N.C.A.A. basketball Final Four with Turner Media, will then have the rights to show both championships in 2021 (Steinberg 2019).

Ticket prices for the game have risen dramatically since Super Bowl I reaching an average face value of over $1,000 per ticket in 2020. The game is popular and tickets are so much in demand that the NFL now controls the entire distribution of tickets. No tickets in the primary market are made available to the general public, with the exception of handicapped seating which is distributed through a league-wide lottery (Roos and Klosowski 2010). Each team playing in the game is allocated 17.5%

[4] Such is the status of the game that even the commercials can become national phenomena. The famous "1984" Apple ad, directed by Oscar nominated director Ridley Scott, aired just once during Super Bowl XVIII, but is widely credited as ushering in an age of elaborate Super Bowl commercials and has been the subject of numerous homages over the years ranging from the popular television show Futurama to the video game Fortnite (Hiltzik 2017). The tagline "Where's the Beef" from a Wendy's commercial from the same year became such a popular national catchphrase (or overused cliché depending on your particular point of view) that it made it into the Democratic presidential primary debate between Vice President Walter Mondale and Senator Gary Hart later that year.

of the tickets, 5% of the tickets go to the host team, and 34.8% are distributed to the other NFL teams (1.2% per team) (Breech 2020). The NFL maintains control of the remaining 25.2% of the tickets which are sold to sponsors, partners, and networks.

Besides ticket prices and distribution, the location of the game is also determined by the NFL. In the earlier years of the game, the NFL would ask cities to bid to host the game. A selection committee would then screen those initial bids, select finalists, and the NFL owners would vote on the final selection (Shallow 2019). That bidding process is no longer used. Now, the NFL selects a city and then asks if they would like to host the game. If the city accepts that offer, the two sides then negotiate the details of the agreement (Shallow 2019). These arrangements are done years prior to the playing of the game. For example, the selection of Miami to host the 2020 game was made in 2016 (Shallow 2019) and as of late 2020, the host has been set through 2024. This lead time gives the host cities years to prepare and also years to observe how other cities host the game.

All in all, it is clear that the Super Bowl is a massive event and is big business. The remainder of this book will examine how this economic activity plays out for the individuals involved. It will explore the impact that playing in the game has on the playing careers of those involved, the impact of being the halftime performer has on earnings, and the degree to which hosting the game is beneficial to the host city.

References

Braunwart, B., & Carroll, B. (1984). Blondy Wallace and the Biggest Football Scandal Ever. *Pro Football Researchers Association, 5*, 1–16.

Breech, J. (2020, January 23). Super Bowl 2020: Chiefs and 49ers Will Get 35 Percent of Tickets, Here's How the Rest Are Distributed. *CBS Sports*. Retrieved from https://www.cbssports.com/nfl/news/super-bowl-2020-chiefs-and-49ers-will-get-35-percent-of-tickets-heres-how-the-rest-are-distri buted/.

Crepeau, R. C. (2014). *NFL Football: A History of America's New National Pastime*. Urbana: University of Illinois Press.

Felser, L. (2008). *The Birth of the New NFL: How the 1966 NFL/AFL Merger Transformed Pro Football*. Guilford, CT: The Lyons Press.

Hartmann, W. R. & Klapper, D. (2017). Super Bowl Ads. *Marketing Science, 37*(1), 78–96.

Hiltzik, M. (2017, January 25). A Reminder That Apple's '1984' Ad Is the Only Great Super Bowl Commercial Ever—And It's Now 33 Years Old. *Los Angeles Times*. Retrieved from https://www.latimes.com/business/hiltzik/la-fi-hiltzik-1984-super-bowl-20170125-story.html.

Kerschbaumer, K. (2020, January 28). Super Bowl LIV: Inside the Numbers. *Sports Video Group*. Retrieved from https://www.sportsvideo.org/2020/01/28/super-bowl-liv-inside-the-numbers/.

Leeds, M., Von Allmen, P., & Matheson, V. (2018). *The Economics of Sports* (6th ed.). New York, NY: Routledge.

MacCambridge, M. (2005). *America's Game: The Epic Story of How Pro Football Captured a Nation*. New York, NY: Anchor Books.

NFL History. (2020). *Super Bowl Winners. ESPN*. Retrieved from http://www.espn.com/nfl/superbowl/history/winners.

Pro Football Hall of Fame. (2020). Birth of Pro Football. *Pro Football Hall of Fame*. Retrieved from https://www.profootballhof.com/football-history/birth-of-pro-football/.

Remember the AFL. (2020). *Minority Players and the American Football League*. Retrieved from http://www.remembertheafl.com/MinorityPlayers.htm.

Roos, D., & Klosowski, T. (2010, October 13). How to Get Super Bowl Tickets. *HowStuffWorks*. Retrieved from https://entertainment.howstuffworks.com/how-to-get-super-bowl-tickets.htm.

Ross, C. (1999). *Outside the Lines: African Americans and the Integration of the National Football League*. New York: New York University Press.

Shallow, L. (2019, February 1). How Does the NFL Pick Super Bowl Cities? *CNN*. Retrieved from https://www.cnn.com/2019/02/01/us/how-nfl-picks-super-bowl-cities/index.html.

Steinberg, B. (2019, March 13). CBS, NBC to Swap Super Bowl Broadcasts. *Variety*. Retrieved from https://variety.com/2019/tv/news/cbs-nbc-swap-super-bowl-1203162667/.

Stewart, M. (2002). *The Super Bowl*. New York, NY: Franklin Press.

Surdam, D. G. (2013). *Run to Glory and Profits: The Economic Rise of the NFL During the 1950s*. Lincoln: University of Nebraska Press.

Veblen, T. (2009). *Theory of the Leisure Class*. Oxford, UK: Oxford University Press.

CHAPTER 3

The Cities

Abstract The Super Bowl is America's premier sporting event. This chapter details basic economic facts about the game and examines the controversy surrounding the purported economic impact of the game on host communities. While the league and sports boosters claim that the game brings up to a $500 million economic impact to host cities, a review of the literature suggests that the true economic impact is a fraction of this amount.

Keywords Sports · Stadiums · Super Bowl · Impact analysis · Football

The Super Bowl is by any measure the most significant annual sporting event in the United States.[1] The game routinely attracts a sellout audience willing to pay top dollar for seats. Super Bowl tickets are among the most expensive in the sports world with average face values that exceeded $1,000 in 2020. And as can be seen in Fig. 3.1, prices have risen dramatically over the years.

Of course, since the NFL and its teams control all of the tickets, without some sort of inside connection, the typical fan would need to go

[1] Parts of this chapter draw from Victor Matheson, "Economics of the Super Bowl," in L. Kahane & S. Shmanske (Eds.), *The Oxford Handbook of Sports Economics, Volume 1* (pp. 470–484). London: Oxford University Press, 2012.

Y. J. Kelly et al., *The Economics of the Super Bowl*, Palgrave Pivots in Sports Economics, https://doi.org/10.1007/978-3-030-46370-0_3

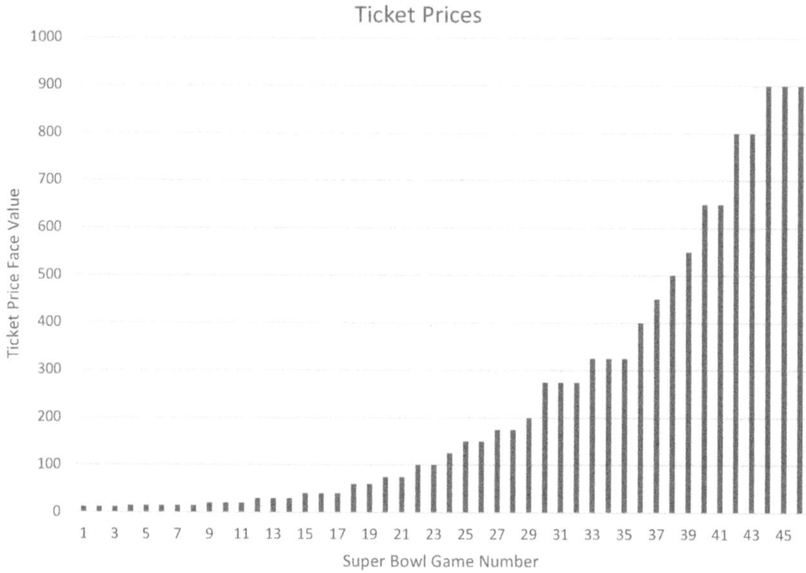

Fig. 3.1 Super Bowl tickets over time

to the secondary market to buy a ticket, and these resellers could expect to receive many times the face value figure in the secondary market. This market is where the news stories originate about the dramatically high price of tickets to the game (as if a face value of $1,000 isn't dramatically high enough on its own). In February 2020, Super Bowl LIV set an American sporting event record with an average secondary market price of nearly $9,000 per ticket (Becker 2020) with some sales exceeding $10,000 (Buchwald 2020).

Table 3.1 shows the average price for a Super Bowl ticket sold on StubHub, a large secondary market dealer, between 2003 and 2020.

The Super Bowl's television viewing numbers are even more impressive. The Super Bowl is far and away the most watched television program in the United States every year. As seen in Fig. 3.2, the Super Bowl experienced rapid growth between its inception and the mid-1980s. Viewership has remained high with the average Super Bowl attracting just under 100 million viewers in the United States between 2000 and 2020 (Nielsen Media Research 2020).

Table 3.1 Average Super Bowl secondary market ticket price

Date	*Matchup*	*Average resale ticket Price*
February 2, 2020	Kansas City Chiefs v. San Francisco 49ers	$8,484
February 3, 2019	New England Patriots v. Los Angeles Rams	$6,612
February 4, 2018	Philadelphia Eagles v. New England Patriots	$5,889
February 5, 2017	New England Patriots v. Atlanta Falcons	$4,628
February 7, 2016	Denver Broncos v. Carolina Panthers	$5,140
February 1, 2015	New England Patriots v. Seattle Seahawks	$6,140
February 2, 2014	Seattle Seahawks v. Denver Broncos	$3,238
February 3, 2013	Baltimore Ravens v. San Francisco 49ers	$2,950
February 5, 2012	New York Giants v. New England Patriots	$3,981
February 6, 2011	Green Bay Packers v. Pittsburgh Steelers	$3,429
February 7, 2010	New Orleans Saints v. Indianapolis Colts	$2,713
February 1, 2009	Pittsburgh Steelers v. Arizona Cardinals	$2,402
February 3, 2008	New England Patriots v. New York Giants	$3,536
February 4, 2007	Indianapolis Colts v. Chicago Bears	$4,004
February 5, 2006	Pittsburgh Steelers v. Seattle Seahawks	$3,009
February 6, 2005	Philadelphia Eagles v. New England Patriots	$2,659
February 1, 2004	New England Patriots v. Carolina Panthers	$2,290
January 26, 2003	Oakland Raiders v. Tampa Bay Buccaneers	$767

Source Slingland (2019) and Rovell (2008)

The relative number of Super Bowl viewers compared to other television programming is even more astounding. For example, 29 of the 30 most watched programs in US television history are Super Bowls, and more recently, the last 21 Super Bowls since the year 2000 are the 21 most watched programs in the United States during the twenty-first century. By way of comparison, over the same period the National Basketball Association (NBA) finals drew 15.9 million per game, Major League

Fig. 3.2 Super Bowl television viewership over time

Baseball's (MLB) the World Series attracted an audience of just over 17.5 million per game, and the National Hockey League's (NHL) Stanley Cup drew a paltry 4.4 million viewers per game. The Super Bowl's television ratings also dwarf non-sports programming. The Academy Awards drew an average of 37.3 million viewers over the same time period, and even the top-rated non-football program since 2000, the series finale of *Friends*, attracted only 52.5 million fans, barely half that of the typical Super Bowl. More recently, the wildly popular *Game of Thrones*' record-setting finale managed an audience of only 19.3 million (Porter 2019). See Table 3.2 for a comparison of television ratings for various sporting and non-sporting events.

It should be noted that we focus solely on American television viewing audiences here. Numerous other sporting events around the world including soccer's annual Champions League final as well as international events such as championship matches of both the soccer and

Table 3.2 Average television audiences for various programming

Event	*Years*	*Rating*	*Share*	*Viewers*
Super Bowl	2000–2020	43.5	66.1	99,713,000
World Series	2000–2019	10.7	n.a.	17,506,000
NBA Finals	2000–2019	9.8	n.a.	15,896,000
Stanley Cup	2000–2019	2.6	n.a.	4,411,000
BCS Championship	2000–2020	15.7	n.a.	26,866,000
Academy Awards	2000–2020	n.a.	n.a.	37,311,000
American Idol Finale	2002–2020	n.a.	n.a.	22,642,000
Friends Finale	2004	29.8	43.0	52,500,000

Note "Rating" is the percentage of households with a television tuned to a particular program. "Share" is the percentage of households currently watching television tuned to a particular program
Source Neilsen Media Research (2020) and various media sources

cricket World Cups and the opening ceremonies of the Summer and Winter Olympic Games likely attract worldwide audiences that exceed those of the Super Bowl. Similarly, the Super Bowl itself attracts sports fans outside the United States with an estimated viewership as high as 40 million international viewers (Margolis 2019). However, television ratings in many countries around the world are not calculated using the same methodology or with the same rigor as is done domestically, and international television ratings are notorious for exaggerating the real number of viewers for special events, especially when sporting organizations such as the International Olympic Committee (IOC) or the Fédération Internationale de Football Association (FIFA) are the ones aggregating the viewership numbers. Given the lack of trustworthy television viewing data on other major sporting events, we omit them here.

Of course, sky-high television ratings also mean sky-high advertising revenues. A 30-second television spot during the Super Bowl is the single most valuable piece of real estate in all of American broadcast television. In 2020, a 30-second commercial during the Super Bowl sold for \$5.6 million, a 6.4% increase on the previous year and a whopping 700% increase since 1990 (Crupi 2019). As shown in Table 3.3, advertising rates at the Super Bowl have experienced a rapid increase over the past two decades, far outpacing inflation as well as the advertising rates for other programming such as the Academy Awards, often considered the non-sports counterpart to the Super Bowl.

Table 3.3 Super Bowl and Academy Awards 30-second advertising spot prices

Year	*Super Bowl ad price*	*Real price (2020 $)*	*% change*	*Academy Awards ad price*	*Real price (2020 $)*	*% change*
1990	$700,400	$1,386,331	n.a.	$450,000	$890,704	n.a.
1991	$800,000	$1,519,530	9.6	n.a.	n.a.	n.a.
1992	$850,000	$1,567,320	3.1	n.a.	n.a	n.a.
1993	$850,000	$1,521,765	−2.9	$607,800	$1,088,151	n.a.
1994	$900,000	$1,571,053	3.2	$643,500	$1,123,303	3.2
1995	$1,150,000	$1,952,133	24.3	$700,000	$1,188,255	5.8
1996	$1,085,000	$1,788,971	−8.4	$705,000	$1,310,813	10.3
1997	$1,200,000	$1,934,206	8.1	$850,000	$1,370,062	4.5
1998	$1,291,100	$2,049,126	5.9	$950,000	$1,507,761	10.1
1999	$1,600,000	$2,484,514	21.2	$1,000,000	$1,552,821	3.0
2000	$2,100,000	$3,154,878	27.0	$1,305,000	$1,960,531	26.3
2001	$2,200,000	$3,213,665	1.9	$1,450,000	$2,118,097	8.0
2002	$2,200,000	$3,163,646	−1.6	$1,290,000	$1,855,047	−12.4
2003	$2,200,000	$3,093,152	−2.2	$1,345,800	$1,892,166	2.0
2004	$2,302,200	$3,152,881	1.9	$1,503,100	$2,058,507	8.8
2005	$2,400,000	$3,179,109	0.8	$1,503,000	$1,990,917	−3.3
2006	$2,500,000	$3,208,085	0.9	$1,646,800	$2,113,230	6.1
2007	$2,385,365	$2,976,242	−7.2	$1,665,800	$2,078,434	−1.6
2008	$2,699,963	$3,244,219	9.0	$1,820,000	$2,186,874	5.2
2009	$3,000,000	$3,617,507	11.5	$1,300,000	$1,567,586	−28.3
2010	$2,800,000	$3,321,838	−8.2	$1,126,700	$1,336,684	−14.7
2011	$2,948,649	$3,391,195	2.1	$1,368,400	$1,573,776	17.7
2012	$3,442,752	$3,879,195	14.4	$1,610,000	$1,814,102	15.3
2013	$3,765,130	$4,181,197	7.8	$1,650,000	$1,832,334	1.0
2014	$4,084,864	$4,463,851	6.8	$1,760,000	$1,923,290	5.0
2015	$4,283,129	$4,674,962	4.7	$1,830,000	$1,997,414	3.9
2016	$4,800,000	$5,173,849	10.7	$1,720,000	$1,853,963	−7.2
2017	$5,399,873	$5,699,034	10.2	$1,910,000	$2,015,817	8.7
2018	$5,235,379	$5,393,687	−5.4	$2,100,000	$2,163,500	7.3
2019	$5,199,916	$5,261,809	−2.4	$1,980,00	$2,003,567	−7.4
2020	$5,600,000	$5,600,000	6.4	$1,980,000	$1,980,000	−1.2

Source Advertising Age online (2009), TNS Media Intelligence (2009), Su and Mc Dowell (2020), and various media sources

How Much Does the NFL make on the Super Bowl?

The popularity of the Super Bowl also makes it wildly profitable for the NFL. The league does not breakout specific estimates for its earnings related to the Super Bowl, but several numbers can be inferred. The Super

Bowl invariably plays to a sold out crowd at a major stadium. As noted previously, the NFL distributes roughly 17.5% of the available tickets to each participating team, 1.2% of the tickets to each non-participating team, and 5% of the tickets to the host team. These teams then distribute their ticket allotments in a variety of ways including possible sale of the tickets to season ticket holders, players, administrators, or other people affiliated with the teams. The remaining quarter of the available tickets are retained by the NFL and distributed to sponsors, the broadcast networks, media, VIPs, and the host committee (Tampa Bay Super Bowl Host Committee 2009). Since a significant portion of the tickets to the Super Bowl are not purchased directly but rather distributed to corporate sponsors or other entities, the NFL and its teams do not fully capture the revenue of the ticket sales, and instead the implicit value of the tickets is incorporated in the value of the sponsorships and licensing deals the league and teams have with these firms. But given the current face value of tickets, which in 2020 ranged from $950 to $5000, just the direct plus the implied ticket revenue of a sold out 75,000 seat stadium is in excess of $100 million.

The rights to broadcast the Super Bowl are not separately sold to broadcasters but are included as part of the multiyear television contracts negotiated with the individual broadcasters with the rights rotating between FOX, CBS, and NBC on a three-year cycle. In 2019, these three broadcasters paid the NFL a combined total of $3.05 billion in licensing fees for the right to broadcast Sunday regular season games, plus a portion of the playoffs, and one Super Bowl every three years (Young 2019). The value of the Super Bowl makes up a significant portion of the value of these rights to these three broadcasters. In 2020, Fox reportedly sold 82 30-second commercials at an average price of $5.6 million during the game for a total of roughly $450 million (McCluskey and Greenspan 2020). Finally, the NFL earns money from licensed Super Bowl products, official sponsors, and from ancillary spending around the Super Bowl including parking, transportation, and concessions. The NFL also earns money from the "Super Bowl Experience," an interactive event featuring football themed activities including autograph sessions, meet-and-greet opportunities, and memorabilia displays, that can attract up to 100,000 visitors each paying a minimum entry fee of $20. The NFL's contract with the host city generally grants the league the right to a significant portion of the event's concession and parking revenues and often provides the league exclusivity regarding game day transportation. For example, the

2014 Super Bowl in New York/New Jersey, required attendees to either purchase a parking pass at a cost of $150 or take an NFL-sponsored bus or train at a cost of $51. Taxi and riding-sharing drop-offs were prohibited as were hotel or restaurant shuttle services (Roth 2014). All in all, ancillary revenues earned by the NFL from the event could easily exceed $10 million.

Economic Impact of the Super Bowl

Of course, it is not just the NFL that might benefit from the Super Bowl. While the spectacle of the big game may be of the greatest interest to the media, marketing experts, and the general public, the overall economic impact of the Super Bowl on host cities has attracted the most interest from academic economists. Unlike championships in the NBA, NHL, and MLB, the Super Bowl takes place at a neutral site rather than being hosted by one of the participating teams. Furthermore, unlike the major bowl games played in college football, the location of the game changes from year to year. In this sense, the Super Bowl is most similar to major international competitions such as the Olympics or World Cup. The Union of European Football Association's (UEFA) annual Champions League final, the biggest annual single day sporting event in Europe, also plays at rotating neutral sites in the same fashion. In the United States, the NCAA's Final Four as well as golf's US Open and PGA Championship are also played in different locations not associated with a particular team or player in the event.

This feature also makes the Super Bowl appealing to analyze from an econometric standpoint. When an event is always in the same place year after year it is hard to disentangle the effect of the event from the underlying attributes of the region in which the event takes place. For example, the Rose Bowl, college football's oldest and one of its most prestigious bowl games, is played every year on or around January 1 in Pasadena, California. Even if one noticed a clear pattern of increased economic activity in Pasadena every January 1, it would not be clear whether the game was responsible for this increase or whether the surge in economic activity was tied to seasonal patterns such as New Year's Day parties or post-Christmas shopping. Since the Super Bowl changes location every year, one can essentially compare the economy during the year of the Super Bowl to the same time period in the previous or following years.

The NFL and league boosters typically claim that the Super Bowl generates huge economic windfalls for the cities lucky enough to be selected as the host for the event. For example, a joint study conducted by the National Football League and the W.P. Carey MBA Sports Business Program estimated an economic impact of $720 million ($786 million in 2020 dollars) from Super Bowl XLIX on the greater Phoenix economy in 2015 (W.P. Carey Business School 2015). As noted by Baade and Matheson (2006a), “If those (types of) numbers are accurate, ‘Super’ is an apt adjective for the event.” Few other events outside of the Olympic Games or soccer’s World Cup can generate such lofty claims of an economic windfall from such a short-term event.

The W.P. Carey MBA Sports Business Program is not alone in their heady claims. Consulting firms, local visitor and tourism bureaus, as well as teams and the league, annually publish eye-popping estimates of the economic impact of the big game and have done so for decades. For example, an NFL-Sports Management Research Institute (SMRI) study attributed a $670 million ($1.04 billion in 2020 dollars) increase in taxable sales in South Florida (Miami-Dade, Broward, and Palm Beach counties) and an increase in economic activity of $396 million ($614 million in 2020 dollars) to the 1999 event (NFL 1999). As with other economic impact reports, this NFL-commissioned study predicted that a horde of affluent tourists would descend on the three-county area. The NFL-SMRI team reported that the average income of Super Bowl attendees is more than twice that of the average visitor to South Florida during the peak tourist months of January and February ($144,500 compared to $40,000–$80,000), and they spend up to four times as much as the average visitor to South Florida ($400.33 per day compared to $99–$199 per day). As noted by Jim Steeg, the NFL’s Vice President for special events from 1977 to 2005,

> The Super Bowl is the most unique of all special events. Extensive studies by host cities, independent organizations and the NFL all try to predict the economic impact the big game will have on a community. They talk to tens of thousands of attendees, local businessmen, corporate planners, media and local fans – looking to see how they are affected.
>
> These studies have provided irrefutable evidence that a Super Bowl is the most dramatic event in the U.S. Super Bowl patrons are significantly more affluent, spend more and have more spent on them, and influence

Table 3.4 Estimates of *ex ante* economic impact of Super Bowl

Year	*Author*	*City*	*Estimate in millions of $ and (millions of 2020 $)*
1994	Jeffrey Humphreys, Georgia State University	Atlanta	$166 ($289.8)
1999	NFL and Kathleen Davis, Sports Management Research Institute	Miami	$396 ($614.9)
2000	Jason Ader, Bear Stearns	Atlanta	$410 ($616.0)
2003	Super Bowl Host Committee	San Diego	$375 ($527.2)
2006	Lawrence Technological University	Detroit	$302 ($387.5)
2007	PriceWaterhouseCoopers	Miami	$390 ($486.6)
2013	University of New Orleans	New Orleans	$480 ($533.0)
2015	W.P. Carey MBA Sports Business Program	Phoenix	$720 ($785.9)
2018	Rockport Analytics	Minneapolis	$380 ($391.5)

Source Various news sources

> future business in the community more than attendees of any other event or convention held in the U.S. (Steeg 1999)

Table 3.4 summarizes a variety of *ex ante* estimates of the impact of the Super Bowl on the host city's economy.

The Costs of Hosting the Game

There are reasons to be skeptical of such claims, however, since the league has strong financial incentives to publicize studies that report a large financial windfall for host cities. The NFL explicitly uses the lure of the Super Bowl as a carrot to convince otherwise reluctant cities to provide public subsidies for the construction of new playing facilities. For example, back in 2004 just days before Arlington, Texas voters narrowly approved a $325 million tax increase to fund a new stadium for the Dallas Cowboys, NFL commissioner Paul Tagliabue visited the area and suggested that the construction of a new stadium would put the city in a prime position to host an upcoming Super Bowl. It should be noted that the 2004 referendum passed by a relatively thin margin of 55–45 despite the team outspending the stadium subsidy opponents by a factor of 100–1 (over $5 million compared to just over $50,000) (Hickey 2004). Indeed, the new $1.15 billion stadium ($1.575 billion in 2020 dollars) hosted the 2011 Super Bowl. Of course, if the Super Bowl really provides a $400 or $500 million boost to a local economy, then, in effect, the benefits of the game could completely cover the public outlay. This logical reasoning only holds, however, if the big game does, in fact, generate substantial economic benefits. Given the amount of taxpayer money that has been spent on the construction or refurbishment of NFL stadiums since the modern stadium boom began in the late 1980s and early 1990s, obtaining accurate measurements of the economic impact of NFL franchises and mega-events such as the Super Bowl is of significant public policy importance.

Table 3.5 shows the hosts of the Super Bowl from 1967 through 2024. It is interesting to note that during the early years of the game, it was common for the same city to host the game multiple times. Fourteen of the first fifteen games were held in either New Orleans, Miami, or the Los Angeles area. More recently, however, the clear tendency has been to spread out the game. Over the sixteen-year period from 2004 to 2019, thirteen different cities held games, and in nine of these cases (Houston, Detroit, Glendale/Phoenix, Dallas/Arlington, Indianapolis, New York/New Jersey, San Francisco/Santa Clara, Minneapolis, Atlanta) the game was awarded shortly after the construction of a new stadium, and in a tenth (New Orleans) immediately after a major stadium renovation. The total direct cost to the taxpayers for the new stadiums in these Super Bowl hosts totaled over $4.3 billion (in 2020 dollars). There can be little doubt that the NFL would not place its premier event in Minneapolis, Detroit, or Indianapolis except in exchange for a large public subsidy in the form of a new stadium for one of the league's franchises. Of course, with so many cities vying to host the Super Bowl, the reality for most locations is that their new stadium will only hold a single Super Bowl over the useful economic life of the facility. Despite this fact, there are probably at least 10 or 12 cities that now sadly and incorrectly believe they are in the four or five-year rotation schedule for the big game.

Aside from the massive costs of a new stadium, the hosting the game itself along with its surrounding activities can be an expensive affair. The event requires significant spending on public services such as public

Table 3.5 Super Bowl locations 1967–2024

City	*Number*	*Years*
Miami	11	1968, 1969, 1971, 1976, 1979, 1989, 1995, 1999, 2007, 2010, 2020
New Orleans	11	1970, 1972, 1975, 1978, 1981, 1986, 1990, 1997, 2002, 2013, 2024[a]
Los Angeles/Pasadena/Inglewood	8	1967, 1973, 1977, 1980, 1983, 1987, 1993, 2022[a]
Tampa	5	1984, 1991, 2001, 2009, 2021[a]
Phoenix/Tempe/Glendale	4	1996, 2008, 2015, 2023[a]
San Diego	3	1988, 1998, 2003
Houston	3	1974, 2004, 2017
Atlanta	3	1994, 2000, 2019
Detroit/Pontiac	2	1982, 2006
Palo Alto/Santa Clara	2	1985, 2016
Minneapolis	2	1992, 2018
Jacksonville	1	2005
Dallas/Arlington	1	2011
Indianapolis	1	2012
New York/New Jersey	1	2014

[a]Announced

safety and security, EMS services, transportation, and sanitation. Glendale, Arizona estimated additional public safety costs of \$2.5–\$3.5 million for Super Bowl XLIX while Minneapolis reported spending an additional \$1.1 million on transportation services (CBS News 2015; Roper 2018).

The NFL also places heavy demands on host cities for facilities. Besides the obvious need for a stadium for an extended period of time, the league also insists on the use of a major convention center for the Super Bowl Experience, hotels for the NFL leadership and the two participating teams, the rights to tens of thousands of parking spaces throughout the week and on Super Bowl Sunday, and advertising space in local newspapers. The NFL even requires exclusive use of golf courses and bowling alleys for use in NFL charity events for which the NFL will get the credit but for which the host city will pay the price tag.

The NFL also demands tax exemptions from all direct expenditures by the league. Therefore, the host city collects no taxes on the hotels in which NFL executives and teams stay, no taxes from parking spaces sold by the league (parking spaces which have often been provided to the league by the city itself), and no taxes from sale of game tickets. The Minnesota Department of Revenue estimated that these exemptions cost state and local governments $10.3 million in foregone revenues during Super Bowl LII (Roper 2018).

Prior to Minnesota's Super Bowl in 2018, the NFL's bid book with the city was secretly leaked to the press (NFL 2013). It was the first time the public had seen a full accounting of the requirements that the NFL expects from Super Bowl hosts. Notably the 154-page document included the phrase "at no cost to the NFL" nearly 200 times. Admittedly, any complex event is likely to require a detailed contract; however, many of the "asks" by the league bordered on the ludicrous. For example, the NFL demanded that if the cell phone signal strength at the team hotels was not considered adequate, the host committee would be required to install temporary portable cellular towers for the duration of the event. Of course, this installation would be "at no cost to the NFL" (NFL 2013, p. 56).

The total costs facing a typical city vary from year to year and are also generally not widely publicized. Glendale, Arizona reported losing $1.6 million in 2008 (CBS News 2015). San Francisco reported losing nearly $5 million when neighboring Santa Clara hosted the game in 2016 (Draper 2018). Local governments around Miami spent nearly $20 million hosting Super Bowl LIV in 2020 including a $4 million payment directly to the owner of the Miami Dolphins who did not actually materially contribute to hosting the event in any way (Flechas 2019). Minneapolis raised $53 million in private donations to defray a portion of the costs of event and the lost government revenues, although it was unclear it this amount was sufficient to cover all the expenses associated with the game. In addition, local charities noted that due to the high demands for Super Bowl donations, fundraising for other charitable purposes in the region was more challenging than in previous years (Roper 2018).

Challenges in Measuring the Benefits of Hosting the Game

On the surface, measuring the economic impact of a large sporting event is a regularly straightforward task. One simply needs to add up the number of attendees at the game and estimate the average fan's expenditures in connection with the game. For example, in assessing the impact of Super Bowl XXVIII on the City of Atlanta and the State of Georgia, Jeffrey Humphreys (1994) estimated that the event generated 306,680 "visitor days" and that the average per diem expenditures per visitor was $252 to arrive at a direct economic impact from the event of $77 million. The indirect economic impact of an event is calculated by taking the direct impact and applying a multiplier to account for the initial round of expenditures recirculating in the economy. While the magnitude of the multiplier can be affected by a large number of variables including the sectors in which the initial spending takes place and the size of the metropolitan area in which the event occurs, typically for major sporting events, the multiplier effect roughly doubles the size of the initial round of spending. Humphreys estimated the indirect economic impact of the 1994 Super Bowl at $89 million for a total impact from the game of $166 million ($290 million in 2020 dollars).

While this type of *ex ante* prediction of the economic impact of the Super Bowl appears straightforward, in fact there are numerous theoretical difficulties with this method of estimation. Three prominent problems frequently cited by economists are the substitution effect, the crowding out effect, and leakages.

The substitution effect occurs when consumers spend money on a sporting event that would normally have been spent elsewhere in the economy. For example, if a parent buys a child a Kansas City Chiefs 2020 Super Bowl Champions sweatshirt as a Christmas present, it is unlikely that this sweatshirt represents an additional gift but instead will be given in the place of another present. In this case, the Super Bowl has not increased total expenditures on gifts but instead has simply rearranged spending patterns toward sports paraphernalia and away from, say, ugly holiday sweaters. In a broader sense, spending on the Super Bowl by residents of the city hosting the game reduces the money available for these consumers to spend elsewhere in the economy. For this reason, most honest practitioners of economic impact analysis exclude most or all spending by local residents from any final economic impact numbers.

Of course, for mega-events like the Super Bowl, the substitution effect is likely to be much lower than for a regular season game since a much larger percentage of the attendees are from out of town. Since few of the attendees at the game are local residents, the substitution effect is likely to be low. On the other hand, the Super Bowl has become a week-long event with numerous open events for fans that are more accessible to the local population. For example, the longest lines at the Super Bowl Experience are not at the exhibits featuring the two teams actually playing in the Super Bowl but instead those that showcase the local NFL team of the host city suggesting that many of the attendees are local residents. Spending at these events by local residents must be factored out of expenditure estimates in order to obtain an accurate assessment of the net economic impact of the game.

In a strange twist of fate, through 2020 and the first 54 years of the Super Bowl (or the first LIV years, to stay in the true Super Bowl mindset), no team has ever played at home for the Super Bowl.[2] Should a team someday break this long-running curse, as the Minnesota Vikings nearly did in 2018 before losing 38-7 to the eventual Super Bowl Champion Philadelphia Eagles in the NFC title game, this would have a significantly negative economic effect on the host city as spending by visitors would fall when local team supporters purchased tickets to the game displacing travelers to the city. So from an economic standpoint, Vikings fans should really thank their 2017–2018 team for continuing their Super Bowl futility. A local team in the Super Bowl would also likely result in record secondary market prices for Super Bowl tickets as local fans, freed from the hassle and expense of traveling to the host city, would have additional funds to spend on tickets to the big game.

Crowding out, a second source of bias in economic impact reports, occurs when the crowds and congestion associated with a sporting event displaces regular economic activity. While there is no doubt that the Super Bowl attracts large numbers of tourists, it is equally clear that others are dissuaded from visiting Super Bowl host cities during the time period around the game. Indeed, the situation is much like Yogi Berra's famous quote, "No one goes there anymore; it's too crowded." Traditionally, the Super Bowl has been held in warm-weather cities that are popular vacation destinations even when the Super Bowl is not in town. Therefore, even if a city's hotels during a Super Bowl are full to capacity with sports fans, if the hotels would have been 70% occupied anyway, the net effect of the Super Bowl is the incremental 30% of additional rooms that are sold not the entire number of rooms sold to Super Bowl visitors. And indeed, on

[2] If any team is equally likely to make the Super Bowl in a given year, the probability of no team ever playing at home through the first 54 years of the event is an unlikely, but not absurdly low 1.76%.

an annual basis, the average hotel in the nation's major tourist markets is filled to roughly 70% capacity (Smith's Travel Research 2020).

A perfect example of this phenomenon occurred in January 2002 in the aftermath of the September 11 terrorist attacks. The attacks caused the NFL season to be pushed back by one week. Unfortunately, the host city that year, New Orleans, was initially unable to accommodate the Super Bowl on the succeeding weekend because of the presence of a large national auto dealers convention the next week. Only when the convention was moved was it possible to host the Super Bowl on the desired week. Therefore, while the Super Bowl filled every hotel room in the city, a large number of these hotel rooms would have been full of auto dealers even in the absence of the Super Bowl. Therefore, the economic impact of the Super Bowl should only include any hotel rooms sold to sports fans over and above the number of rooms that would have been sold anyway. Of course, holding Super Bowls in cold weather locations such as Detroit, Indianapolis, or Minneapolis is likely to reduce any potential crowding out effects as Minnesota in February tends to be low on most sane person's vacation wish list.

Crowding out may also be less of a problem in a place like New York City which has over 120,000 hotel rooms. With such a large hotel capacity, the city may be able to accommodate both a Super Bowl and a reasonably large percentage of the city's normal tourist population. This should also be kept in mind for a likely future Super Bowl in Las Vegas. In 2020, the Oakland Raiders moved to Las Vegas and into their new $1.8 billion stadium (which included $750 million of public financing championed by the prominent small government promoter and wildly hypocritical Sheldon Adelson). Given the NFL's tendency to award the Super Bowl to cities constructing new stadiums, Las Vegas is a likely site of the next Super Bowl to be awarded for 2025 or soon thereafter. With nearly 150,000 hotel rooms, the city has more lodging capacity than any other city in the world.

The third major consideration is the problem with leakages. While a great deal of money may be spent within a city during a mega-event, much of the money may immediately leak out of the city and not end up in the pockets of local residents. In other words, the event may generate economic activity in the city but not generate income for its citizens. Of course, normal multiplier analysis as performed by software modeling packages such as the Bureau of Economic Analysis' Regional Input–Output Multiplier System (RIMS II) or IMPLAN (IMpact analysis for PLANing) does account for leakages in its modeling. However, the complex input-output matrices upon which these models rely are based on the normal inter-industry relationships that exist in local economies, and during a mega-event these relationships may be anything but normal.

For example, it is common practice for hotels to double or triple their rates during the Super Bowl. Between 2015 and 2019, for example, the average price of a hotel room in downtown Houston near the NRG Stadium was $127.50, but during the 2017 Super Bowl, the average room price hit a record $446.86 per night, an increase of just over 250% (Baumann et al. 2020). Local hotel desk clerks and room cleaners in Houston, however, didn't see a 250% increase in their wages. It was not the local workers but instead executives back at corporate headquarters in New York City and shareholders spread across the world who benefitted from the event. Since a smaller portion of visitor spending at hotels winds up in the hands of local residents during the Super Bowl, multipliers calculated using average spending patterns are likely to be biased upwards (Matheson 2009).

Capacity constraints in cities also lead to leakages. The Super Bowl is a large enough event that many services demanded by visitors, ranging from high-end catering to exotic dancing, cannot be fulfilled solely by local providers. Therefore, labor and capital are often imported into the host city to meet the excess demand. The higher prices that prevail during the Super Bowl may also bring those with an entrepreneurial spirit into the host city. Uber, Lyft, and other ride-sharing services, for example, utilize surge pricing to help manage supply and demand. Drivers anticipating an extended period of surge pricing due to the Super Bowl will commonly come into town for Super Bowl weekend to take advantage of these higher fares. Of course, payments to these imported factors of production do not represent income for the city but instead increase incomes of the guest workers.

Another obvious illustration of this situation occurred in Jacksonville in 2005. Jacksonville was a significantly smaller and less popular tourist destination than Super Bowl venues such as New Orleans or Miami, and the city, therefore, had significantly fewer hotel rooms available than most other host cities. To alleviate the shortage of hotel rooms, the Super Bowl host committee arranged for six large cruise ships to dock in the area, providing housing for up to 7,600 guests (Donovan 2005).

Of course, after the big weekend, the ships pulled up anchor and sailed away, taking any revenues they generated with them. In effect, all spending that occurred on these ships was subject to nearly 100% leakage (an obviously unfortunate term when referring to cruise ships) from the Jacksonville economy.

Other issues that may affect the true net economic impact of an event include casual visitors and time switching. Casual visitors are tourists who attend a sporting event while traveling but whose primary purpose for traveling is not sports related. For example, the authors of this book have frequently attended conferences together.[3] Inevitably, when a group of sports economists gets together, we often seek out a local sporting event to attend. A typical economic impact study would count the spending at the event and perhaps even the spending on that day's lodging by the supply of economists as economic impact generated by the sporting event. However, the sporting event had no influence on whether the economists visited the city, and the spending done at the ballpark simply substitutes away from spending that would have taken place elsewhere in the economy in the absence of the game. Of course, with a huge event like the Super Bowl, casual spending is unlikely to play a significant role since scarce hotel rooms and high lodging prices will preclude large numbers of non-sports fans from being in the city during Super Bowl week anyway.

Time switching, however, may be an important factor when considering the economic impact of the Super Bowl. Time switching occurs when an individual is planning to visit a city but rearranges his or her schedule to coincide with a sporting event. The sporting event does not influence whether the person visits the city but instead only influences the timing. This factor can certainly be important for the Super Bowl. A person may have long desired to visit a tourist destination like New Orleans, and the Super Bowl is what finally prompts the individual to take that trip. But once the sports fan has seen the city, the tourist has crossed the city off of his or her future vacation destinations.

Empirical Studies of the Super Bowl

Given the theoretical shortcomings of traditional economic impact analysis as well as public policy implications of publishing potentially inflated economic benefit numbers, numerous independent scholars not

[3] A group of economists is formally referred to as a "supply of economists."

connected with the NFL or any Super Bowl host committees have examined the *ex post* impact of hosting the Super Bowl on a wide variety of economic variables including employment, personal income, per capita income, taxable sales, tax revenues, hotel spending, and other visitor statistics. In general, these studies have all come to the same conclusion: the Super Bowl generates a fraction the economic impact claimed by boosters.

Porter (1999) examines short-term data on sales receipts for several Super Bowls concluding,

> Investigator bias, data measurement error, changing production relationships, diminishing returns to both scale and variable inputs, and capacity constraints anywhere along the chain of sales relations lead to lower multipliers. Crowding out and price increases by input suppliers in response to higher levels of demand and the tendency of suppliers to lower prices to stimulate sales when demand is weak lead to overestimates of net new sales due to the event. These characteristics alone would suggest that the estimated impact of the mega-sporting event will be lower than the impact analysis predicts.

Baade and Matheson (2000) examine twenty-five Super Bowls from 1973 to 1997 and find that the game is associated with an increase in employment in the host metropolitan area of 537 jobs. Based on simple assumptions regarding the value of a job to a community, they estimate an average economic impact of roughly $30 million ($48.4 million in 2020 dollars) or approximately one-tenth the figures touted by the NFL.

Baade and Matheson (2006a) update their previous results by directly examining personal income in host cities. They find that for Super Bowls held between 1970 and 2001, the host city experienced an average increase in personal income of $91.9 million ($134.2 million in 2020 dollars). While this amount is not statistically significant at any generally accepted level, Baade and Matheson also calculate confidence intervals for their point estimate and conclude that there is less than a 5% probability that the true impact of the Super Bowl on personal incomes in host metropolitan statistical areas exceeds $300 million ($438 million in 2020 dollars), and the chance that the true impact exceeds $400 million ($584 million in 2020 dollars) is less than 1%.

Coates and Humphreys (2002) look at all postseason play in American professional sports, not just the Super Bowl, and find that hosting the

Super Bowl had no statistically significant effect on per capita income in the host city. Interestingly, however, they do find that the city of the winner of the Super Bowl experiences statistically significant increase of roughly $140 in per capita income ($205 in 2020 dollars). They attribute this finding to possible higher labor efficiency due to a "feel-good" effect although they concede that the most likely answer is simply spurious correlation. Matheson (2005), on the other hand, arrives at a figure of between a $50 and $60 (roughly $75 in 2020 dollars) increase in per capita income for winning cities, a figure that is not statistically significantly different from zero at the 5% significance level.

Davis and End (2010) extend the results of both of the previous papers. While their paper focuses on the effects of team winning percentage on citywide wages and income per capita, they include variables for both hosting and winning the Super Bowl. Under various estimation methods the coefficient on winning the Super Bowl is nearly always positive and is statistically significant at the 5% level in roughly half of the estimations. Interestingly, the coefficient on hosting the Super Bowl is nearly always negative and is again statistically significant at the 5% level in roughly half of the regression models suggesting that there is evidence that hosting the Super Bowl may actually have a significant negative impact on income per capita in host cities.

As noted previously, a major difficulty of measuring the economic impact of events like the Super Bowl is that even the effect of largest sporting events may be hard to isolate within the large, diverse metropolitan economies in which they take place. For example, even if the Super Bowl does result in a $500 million boost to the host city, this is less than 0.2% of the annual GDP of a large metropolitan area like Miami, the most frequent Super Bowl host. Any income gains as a result of the big game would likely be obscured by normal fluctuations in the region's economy. This problem is further compounded by the fact that the Super Bowl, even with its surrounding activities, lasts for only a few days. Even if the effects of the event are large in the time period immediately surrounding the Super Bowl, this impact is likely to be obscured in annual data. All of the *ex post* studies described previously utilize annual data.

If a data source that covers a smaller geographical area or a shorter time frame can be uncovered, however, any potential impact is more likely to be identified. For example, while the presence of the Super Bowl might have a large effect on neighborhood businesses, the overall effect on a state or country's economy will be minuscule and hard to identify. Furthermore, these same economic effects may be large for the time period immediately surrounding the event, but over the course of an entire year, the impact of a single week-long period is not likely to show up as an important change.

For this reason, multiple researchers have turned to taxable sales which are often available monthly and frequently cover areas as small as individual cities and counties instead of entire states or metropolitan areas. In other words, if trying to correctly identify the economic impact of the Super Bowl is like trying to find a needle in a haystack, one solution is to simply make the haystack smaller. Furthermore, general sales tax collections or specific increases in the sales tax rate have been used to finance many publicly funded sports facilities making an examination of taxable sales especially relevant from a public policy standpoint. For example, of the 23 new stadiums constructed for NFL franchises between 1992 and 2009, 7 were funded, at least in part, through increases in the local general sales tax rate while another 8 were funded through increased excise taxes, i.e., sales taxes on specific goods and services such as rental cars or hotel rooms (Baade and Matheson 2006b). In addition, the single largest component of gross domestic product is consumer spending, much of which is captured by taxable sales, and therefore taxable sales are a good proxy for overall economic activity.

Baade et al. (2008) examine monthly taxable sales in Florida counties between 1980 and 2005. Three Florida cities (Miami, Tampa, and Jacksonville) hosted seven Super Bowls during this period. Six of the seven Super Bowls show no significant increase in taxable sales during the event, and the authors calculate that a typical game increased taxable sales by roughly $99 million ($131 million in 2020 dollars).

Coates (2006) performs a similar analysis on monthly sales tax collections for the city of Houston finding that the Super Bowl increases tax revenues by roughly $5 million. Coates and Depken (2011) extend this analysis to cover multiple cities in Texas again finding a slightly lower but still statistically significant increase in sales tax revenue associated with hosting the Super Bowl of $3.92 million ($4.71 million in 2020 dollars. Given a tax rate of 5%, this approximates an increase in taxable sales of $78.4 million ($94.2 million in 2020 dollars), confirming the results of Baade et al. (2008).

Interestingly, the NFL itself has also examined the effect of the Super Bowl on taxable sales. In one of the few examples of a league-sponsored *ex post* study, the NFL reported that, "Thanks to Super Bowl XXXIII, there was a $670 million increase in taxable sales in South Florida compared to the equivalent January-February period in 1998" (NFL 1999). Indeed, a cursory examination of the data shows that the three-county region of Miami-Dade, Broward, and Palm Beach counties did experience an increase in taxable sales roughly the size of that claimed by the league. Unfortunately for the NFL, their study is woefully inept as the league neglected to account for factors besides the Super Bowl, such as inflation, population growth, and routine economic expansion, that could account for the rise in taxable sales. As noted as by Baade and Matheson (2000), over 90% of the increase can be accounted for by these variables.

Of further interest is the fact that if taxable sales are further broken down by county, both Broward and Palm Beach counties actually experienced lower than expected taxable sales in 1999 (by $14 and $16 million respectively) despite the presence of the Super Bowl. Only Miami-Dade county (the actual location of the Super Bowl) experienced an increase in taxable sales (of $67 million) beyond expectations. This is further evidence that mega-events merely tend to shift resources from one area to another rather than generating new economic activity.

Finally, it is worth noting that taxable sales in the area during January–February 2000, the year after the game, were $1.26 billion higher than in the same months during the Super Bowl year. Strangely, the NFL never publicized a story announcing, "Thanks to the lack of a Super Bowl, there was a $1.26 billion increase in taxable sales in South Florida compared to the equivalent January- February period in 1999."

The most recent research regarding the Super Bowl by Heller and Stephenson (2020) and Baumann et al. (2020) goes one step further at identifying the needle in the haystack by actually using daily data on hotel stays to estimate economic impact. Baumann et al. (2020) examine hotel rates, revenue, and occupancy in Houston from 2014 to 2018. Super Bowl LI in 2017 has far and away the largest impact on the hotel market in the greater Houston area of any event over that time period raising the total number of rooms sold by a cumulative total of 38,431 rooms over a four-day period around the game, increasing the average occupancy rate by 20 points to roughly 95% capacity, and raising the average hotel room price by $218.21. Overall hotel revenue during this period was nearly $39 million above what normally would have been expected for a February in 2017, an increase of 364%.

While this is no doubt a significant increase, it is relatively small compared to what the boosters often claim. For a typical Super Bowl traveler, game tickets, airfare, and lodging are the three biggest expenditures. Because the NFL claims all of the ticket revenue, and airline tickets are sold by nationally owned airlines with widely dispersed labor forces and stockholders, only hotel spending has any real impact on the economy of the host city. For many travelers, spending on lodging may represent the majority of spending that a person does within the actual city being visited, especially if the visit occurs during a period of abnormally high hotel prices (like during the Super Bowl). So, if the marginal increase in hotel revenues, the single largest spending category affecting the host city's economy and one highly inflated due to abnormally high room rates, is only $39 million, it is nearly impossible to arrive at a total economic impact anywhere near $500 million for the Super Bowl.

Indeed, the analysis of hotel data shows how hopelessly optimistic many economic projections of Super Bowl gains really are. Boosters will commonly assert that the Super Bowl will attract 100,000 visitors. For example, the previously mentioned work of Jeffrey Humphreys (1994), who to be fair provided the least "boosterish" *ex ante* estimate provided in Table 3.4, still assumed that the Super Bowl generated 306,680 "visitor days" in Atlanta in 1994, a number wildly at odds with Baumann et al.'s (2020) finding that fewer than 40,000 additional hotel rooms were sold in Houston in 2017.

And of course, Humphreys is far from the worst offender. Like Alice in Lewis Carroll's *Through the Looking Glass*, some consultants apparently like to "believe as many as six impossible things before breakfast" (Carroll 1871). Prior to the New York/New Jersey Super Bowl in 2014, city officials projected every hotel room in the area would sell out rapidly with as many at 400,000 visitors descending on the city for the event (Prieto 2014). But the New York/New Jersey area is home to over 120,000 hotel rooms while MetLife Stadium holds fewer than 83,000 fans, so unless hundreds of thousands of football fans were going to come to Manhattan just so they could stay in an overpriced hotel, drinking overpriced beer at a New York bar all so they could bask in the reflected glory of a game taking place twenty miles away in another state, there was simply no way these beliefs ever reflected any type of reality. Indeed, four days before the big game, two-thirds of Manhattan hotels had rooms available, and prices had fallen over 30% from their peak (Stapen 2014).

Nonmonetary Benefits

If the monetary benefits of the Super Bowl generally fail to materialize at the level predicted by *ex ante* estimates, it is often claimed that the Super Bowl brings indirect or nonpecuniary benefits to host cities that add substantially to the direct monetary benefits. For example, in assessing the impact Super Bowl XLII in Glendale, Arizona, Michael Mokwa, chair of the marketing department at the W. P. Carey School of Business stated, "'The money is just the tip of the iceberg. Thousands and thousands of people who came here for the Super Bowl, of whom many had never been to the Valley before, took away powerful memories and good feeling about Arizona.' This translates, he said, into coveted return visits, family and business relocations, and word-of-mouth marketing throughout the country. Priceless, as MasterCard is fond of saying" (W.P. Carey School of Business 2008).

Alan Sanderson, a University of Chicago economist counters, however, that anyone who claims that the intangible benefits of an event like the Super Bowl are "priceless" or "immeasurable" either are "too lazy to go find the correct answer or are afraid of what the true answer might be."

Certainly the game brings potential intangible benefits to the host city. The game can serve to advertise the city to future conventions, businesses, and individual tourists. But here too, estimates of potential benefits can be inflated by the league. First, while word-of-mouth stories are generally considered the single most effective advertising tool for cities' hospitality industries, sporting events may generate a significantly different type of message for potential future tourists than regular vacations or business trips (Zimbalist 2015). A non-sports traveler may return from New Orleans and rave to his or her friends and family about the beignets at Café du Monde, the music on Bourbon Street, and the Corona and hurricanes (the drinks, not the disaster that was 2020). These discussions have the distinct possibility of leading those hearing about the attractions New Orleans has to offer to plan their own visit to the city. This is exactly the sort of "coveted return visits" noted by Professor Mokwa previously.

A football fan visiting New Orleans for the Super Bowl is also likely to bring tales of their trip back to their colleagues. But these might be stories of getting to see the Lombardi trophy, meeting famous NFL coach and announcer John Madden in a hole in the wall Chinese restaurant (as one of the authors did during the 1992 Super Bowl in Minneapolis while he was in grad school at the University of Minnesota), watching Prince give the most spectacular halftime show in Super Bowl history (this fact is not up to debate), or seeing, in person, David Tyree making the most unbelievable catch in Super Bowl history to lead the New York Giants over the New England Patriots in Super Bowl XLII (sorry for the reminder, Patriots fans.) In this case, these stories may also spur those listening to want to experience a trip like this. However, that "coveted return visit" is not to New Orleans but is instead to the next Super Bowl destination. And in fact, by crowding out regular visitors, who might generate future visits to the host city through their discussions with acquaintances with sports fans who instead generate future visits to future Super Bowl host cities, the Super Bowl may actually reduce future tourism.

Other methods of estimating the advertising value of the Super Bowl to the host city are also questionable. Overhead television shots of the stadium or its surroundings broadcast during the game are often assigned a value at the same rate as commercial advertising during the game. Thus, a 30-second shot of Hard Rock Stadium just outside downtown Miami is valued at the same rate as a regular 30-second commercial spot, which sold for $5.6 million in 2020. Given the large number of times the stadium or the city is shown during the game, such advertising can easily add up to tens or hundreds of millions of dollars of imputed value. But such calculations must be flatly incorrect.

First, this technique implies that a simple 30-second overhead shot has the same effect on the consumer as a targeted and professionally designed commercial. Such an implication is both wildly improbable and would invalidate the *raison d'être* of the entire advertising industry. Next, this technique assumes that advertising the city is not subject to diminishing marginal returns. While the first shot of the city may have an advertising effect, it is almost certainly not the case that the thirtieth panoramic scene would have the same impact. Finally, when city tourism bureaus state that the Super Bowl provides more advertising for a city than the city would be able to purchase on its own, in fact revealed preference suggests that the game provides more advertising than the city would be *willing* to purchase on its own. The very fact that cities rarely have tourism advertising budgets in the hundreds of millions of dollars suggests that cities typically don't value such advertising very highly.

There are several other considerations that should be mentioned. First, while the Super Bowl may generate some repeat visitors, if time switching is occurring, as discussed previously the Super Bowl may actually lead to less future tourism. Next, while it is frequently claimed that mega-events like the Super Bowl serve to "put a city on the map," most Super Bowl hosts are large, popular tourist destinations that are already homes to multiple Fortune 500 corporate headquarters and are frequent convention sites. By any definition, cities like Miami, New Orleans, and Los Angeles are already on everyone's map.

Groothuis and Rotthoff (2016) find that the Super Bowl doesn't even result in a particularly strong advertising effect. In a questionnaire designed ascertain the effect of mega-events on civic pride, only 22.7% of all survey respondents could identify where last year's Super Bowl was held and even only 36.1% of people who follow sports very closely remembered the game's previous location. In addition, fewer than a quarter of respondents suggested that hosting the Super Bowl made them more interested in the host city, and just 17.5% stated that hosting the Super Bowl would make them want to visit the city after the event.

Furthermore, not every host city comes away from the game with an enhanced reputation. Many visitors left Jacksonville, the host of Super Bowl XXXIX, with the impression that the city had little to offer in the way of excitement or cultural amenities. In 2011, the Dallas/Arlington, Texas Super Bowl was hit with a paralyzing ice storm showcasing the area's distinct comparative disadvantage over true warm-weather destinations like New Orleans or Miami. New York/New Jersey's 2014 game was plagued by massive transportation delays. And in 2013, Super Bowl XLVII, which was supposed to highlight New Orleans' resiliency and recovery from the devastation of Hurricane Katrina eight years prior, instead highlighted the fact that the city couldn't even manage to keep the lights on during the biggest event of the year as the game suffered a 34-minute delay due to a power outage during the middle of the third quarter (CBS News 2013). Finally, while no Super Bowl has ever suffered from an incident of terrorism or mass violence, as America's premier event, hosting the game does place a bullseye on the city, and the reputations of Munich, Germany, and Atlanta, Georgia still suffer from the terrorist events that took place in their cities during previous Olympic Games.

As for business movement prompted by hosting a major event, while it is possible that a company could decide to locate its corporate headquarters or production facilities to a new city based on the favorable impressions its CEO or other executives had while in town for the Super Bowl, there isn't even anecdotal evidence of any major corporate relocations associated with this or any other mega-sporting event. While there is no denying that intangible benefits from the Super Bowl may exist, there does not appear to be much empirical evidence that they are very large.

Several studies have tried to measure the impact of the Super Bowl on factors besides direct spending during Super Bowl weekend. Coates and Matheson (2011) examine rental housing prices before, during, and after the Super Bowl with the idea that if the Super Bowl represents a valuable amenity for local residents (or an opportunity for renters or landlords to make money through subletting their apartments through a service like Airbnb), this should be reflected in rental prices. Their analysis of rental prices in a panel of American cities from 1993 to 2005 fails to find a consistent impact of the Super Bowl on rental prices, and conclude that the game is as likely to reduce rental prices as increase them.

Baumann et al. (2012) examine the effect of the Super Bowl on crime rates in various cities. Using the Federal Bureau of Investigation's Uniform Crime Reports (UCR) county-level data from 1981 to 2006, they find that hosting the Super Bowl has no effect on property crime. However, hosting the game has a statistically significant effect on violent crime, reducing incidents by 17.5 per 100,000 people, a decrease of about 2.5%. The authors suggest that because the site of the Super Bowl is known years in advance, local law enforcement agencies may take steps to "clean up the town" for their city's big moment in the spotlight and that these efforts at crime eradication may persist for some time after the event is over.

Finally, there is evidence that mega-events may lead to a "feel-good" effect for local residents and instill a measure of civic pride in the host city. Kim and Walker (2012) surveyed local residents after Super Bowl XLIII in 2009 in Tampa, Florida. They found large majorities of respondents reported enhanced community pride and attachment and excitement surrounding the event. For example, 86% reported an increase in a sense of well-being, 84% reported heightened self-respect for the community, 78% stated that they thought the event enhanced the image of their community as a major city, and 77% thought the event brought excitement to the community. These results are in line with the findings about other mega-events such as the Olympics and World Cup (Maennig and Porsche 2008). That being said, it is difficult to place a reasonable monetary value of this temporary feel-good effect, and it remains safe to say that the Super Bowl may make a city happy, but it is unlikely to make a city rich.

Conclusion

There is little doubt that the Super Bowl is at the center of the American sports universe. It is the most watched sporting event, or any event for that matter, in the country every year. The game also has the highest priced tickets and the most expensive sponsorships among spectator sports. If one believes the *ex ante* estimates of economic impact provided by the NFL and civic boosters, the event also generates many hundreds of millions of dollars in benefits for the host city, and the league uses these promises of riches to convince cities that the construction of a new NFL stadium at significant public expense is a profitable investment, especially if it includes the promise of a future Super Bowl.

Because lure of the Super Bowl is used to extract public financing from cities, however, this creates ample reason to be skeptical of any claims made about the reported economic impact since the sponsors of the impact studies have a financial interest in results that show large economic benefits from the game. Aside from the inherent incentive problem associated with impact assessments, there are numerous theoretical reasons to be wary of economic impact statements. Such reports do a notoriously poor job of accounting for the substitution effect and the crowding out effect. In short, while *ex ante* economic impact studies often do a good job measuring activity that *does* occur because of an event, they do a poor job at measuring any economic activity that *does not* occur because of an event. In other words, economic impact studies typically measure gross economic activity when what is really desired is a measure of net economic activity. Furthermore, standard multiplier analysis may give misleading and inflated results when applied during mega-events.

Ex post economic analyses of the Super Bowl by scholars not financially connected with the game have typically found that the observed effects of the game on real economic variables such as employment, government revenues, taxable sales, GDP, hotel stays, and personal income, while generally positive, are a fraction of those claimed by the league and sports boosters. When considering optimal public policy with respect to sports infrastructure, it would be wise to take any claims of super benefits from the Super Bowl with a grain of salt. It appears that most economic impact reports are "padded" at least as well as the players on the field.

References

Advertising Age. (2009). *Super Bowl 2007—Advertising History: 40 Years of Prices and Audience*. http://adage.com/SuperBowlBuyers/superbowlhistory07.html. Accessed November 15, 2009.

Baade, R., Baumann, R., & Matheson, V. (2008). Selling the Game: Estimating the Economic Impact of Professional Sports Through Taxable Sales. *Southern Economic Journal, 74*, 794–810.

Baade, R., & Matheson, V. (2000). An Assessment of the Economic Impact of the American Football Championship, the Super Bowl, on Host Communities. *Reflets et Perspectives, 30*, 35–46.

Baade, R., & Matheson, V. (2006a). Padding Required: Assessing the Economic Impact of the Super Bowl. *European Sports Management Quarterly, 6*, 353–374.

Baade, R., & Matheson, V. (2006b). Have Public Finance Principles Been Shut Out in Financing New Stadiums for the NFL? *Public Finance and Management, 6*, 284–320.

Baumann, R., Ciavarra, T., Englehardt, B., & Matheson, V. A. (2012). Sports Franchises, Events, and City Livability: An Examination of Spectator Sports and Crime Rates. *Economics and Labour Relations Review, 23*(2), 83–97.

Baumann, R., Matheson, V., & Stephenson, E. F. (2020). *Comparing the Visitor Impact of Sporting Events vs. Cultural Events: Evidence from Hotel Data* (Department of Economics and Accounting Working Paper Series). College of the Holy Cross.

Becker, J. (2020, January 20). Super Bowl LIC: 49ers-Chiefs Tickets Going for Record Amount on Secondary Market, *San Jose Mercury News*. https://www.mercurynews.com/2020/01/19/super-bowl-liv-49ers-chiefs-tickets-going-for-record-amount-on-secondary-market/,m.

Buchwald, E. (2020, January 22). Super Bowl 2020 Tickets Now Cost an Average of $10,000. *Market Watch*. Retrieved from https://www.marketwatch.com/story/super-bowl-ticket-prices-nearing-9000-heres-whats-driving-the-cost-2020-01-22.

Carroll, L. (1871). *Through the Looking Glass*.

CBS News. (2013. February 4). Super Bowl Power Outage: What Went Wrong? *CBS News*. https://www.cbsnews.com/news/super-bowl-power-outage-what-went-wrong/.

CBS News. (2015, January 24). Super Bowl's Arizona Host May Be on the Hook for Millions. CBS News. https://www.cbsnews.com/news/super-bowl-2015-host-city-in-arizona-may-be-on-the-hook-for-millions/.

Coates, D. (2006). The Tax Benefits of Hosting the Super Bowl and the MLB All-Star Game: The Houston Experience. *International Journal of Sport Finance, 1*, 239–252.

Coates, D., & Depken, C. A., II. (2011). Mega-Events: Is Baylor Football to Waco What the Super Bowl Is to Houston? *Journal of Sports Economics, 12*(6), 599–620.

Coates, D., & Humphreys, B. (2002). The Economic Impact of Post-season Play in Professional Sports. *Journal of Sports Economics, 3,* 291–299.

Coates, D., & Matheson, V. (2011). Mega-Events and Housing Costs: Raising the Rent While Raising the Roof? *Annals of Regional Science, 46,* 119–137.

Crupi, A. (2019, November 25). Fox Sell Out Its Super Bowl Inventory. *Ad Age*. https://adage.com/article/special-report-super-bowl/fox-sells-out-its-super-bowl-liv-commercial-inventory/2218411.

Davis, M. C., & End, C. M. (2010). A Winning Proposition: The Economic Impact of Successful National Football League Franchises. *Economic Inquiry, 48*(1), 39–50.

Donovan, J. (2005, February 4). From Downtown? Jax's Urban Sprawl Makes for Super Tough Week. *Sports Illustrated Online*. http://sportsillustrated.cnn.com/2005/writers/john_donovan/02/04/scene.jacksonville/.

Draper, K. (2018, January 29). Windfall for Super Bowl Hosts? Economists Say It's Overstated. *New York Times*. https://www.nytimes.com/2018/01/29/sports/football/super-bowl-lii-minnesota.html.

Flechas, J. (2019, August 17). Miami Governments Spending Millions to Make Money and Get Exposure from Super Bowl 54. *Miami Herald*. https://www.miamiherald.com/news/local/community/miami-dade/article234002167.html.

Groothuis, P., & Rotthoff, K. (2016). The Economic Impact and Civic Pride Effects of Sports Teams and Mega-Events: Do the Public and the Professionals Agree? *Economic Affairs, 36*(1), 21–32.

Heller, L., & Stephenson, E. F. (2020, in press). How Does the Super Bowl Affect Host City Tourism? *Journal of Sports Economics*.

Hickey, M. (2004, November 4). Cowboys Stadium Financing Passes in Arlington. *KERA News*. https://www.keranews.org/archive/2004-11-04/cowboys-stadium-financing-passes-in-arlington.

Humphreys, J. (1994, May–June). *The Economic Impact of Hosting Super Bowl XXVIII on Georgia*. Georgia Business and Economic Conditions, 18–21.

Kim, W., & Walker, M. (2012). Measuring the Social Impacts Associated with Super Bowl XLIII: Preliminary Development of a Psychic Income Scale. *Sport Management Review, 15*(1), 91–108.

Maennig, W., & Porsche, M. (2008). The Feel-Good Effect at Mega Sport Events: Recommendations for Public and Private Administration Informed by the Experience of the FIFA World Cup 2006. *Hamburg Contemporary Economic Discussions* 18.

Margolis, J. (2019, February 1). Many International Fans of American Football Are 'Born' on Super Bowl Sunday. *The World*. https://www.pri.org/stories/

2019-02-01/many-international-fans-american-football-are-born-super-bowl-Sunday.
Matheson, V. (2005). Contrary Evidence on the Economic Effect of the Super Bowl on the Victorious City. *Journal of Sports Economics, 6*, 420–428.
Matheson, V. (2009). Economic Multipliers and Mega-Event Analysis. *International Journal of Sport Finance, 4*, 63–70.
McCluskey, M., & Greenspan, R. (2020, February 2). These Were the Best Super Bowl 2020 Commericals. *Time*. https://time.com/5772692/best-super-bowl-commercials-2020/.
National Football League. (1999). Super Bowl XXXII Generates $396 Million for South Florida. *NFL Report*, 58.
National Football League. (2013). *NFL Super Bowl LII Host City Bid Specifications*. https://www.documentcloud.org/documents/1513830-nfl-super-bowl-lii-host-city-bid-specifications.html. Accessed August 25, 2020.
Nielsen Media Research. (2020, February 3). *Historical Super Bowl Viewership*. https://www.nielsen.com/us/en/press-releases/2020/super-bowl-liv-draws-nearly-100-million-tv-viewers-44-million-social-media-interactions/. Accessed July 31, 2020.
Porter, P. (1999). Mega-Sports Events as Municipal Investments: A Critique of Impact Analysis. In J. Fizel, E. Gustafson, & L. Hadley (Eds.), *Sports Economics: Current Research*. Westport, CT: Praeger Press.
Porter, R. (2019, May 20). Game of Thrones' Series Finale Sets All-Time HBO Ratings Record. *Hollywood Reporter*. https://www.hollywoodreporter.com/live-feed/game-thrones-series-finale-sets-all-time-hbo-ratings-record-1212269.
Prieto, B. (2014, January 27). Super Bowl Week Gets Underway: N.Y./N.J. to See Some 400,000 Tourists. *Denver Post*. https://www.denverpost.com/2014/01/27/super-bowl-week-gets-underway-n-y-n-j-to-see-some-400000-tourists/.
Roper, E. (2018, February 3). Cost of Hosting Super Bowl Remains Unclear, but NFL Demands a Lot. *Star Tribune*. https://www.startribune.com/cost-of-hosting-super-bowl-remains-unclear-but-nfl-demands-a-lot/472512273/.
Roth, D. (2014, February 3). The Case of Super Bowl XLVIII vs. New Jersey Transit. *SB Nation*. https://www.sbnation.com/2014/2/3/5372926/the-case-of-super-bowl-xlviii-vs-new-jersey-transit.
Rovell, D. (2008, January 14). Super Bowl Tickets: What They Could Cost This Year. *CNBC*. http://www.cnbc.com/id/22647777. Accessed November 15, 2009.
Slingland, J. (2019, May 27). A Detailed History of Super Bowl Ticket Prices. *TickPick Blog*. https://www.tickpick.com/blog/history-of-super-bowl-ticket-prices/. Accessed July 31, 2020.

Smith's Travel Research. (2020). *U. S. Weekly Hotel Review*. https://str.com/. Accessed August 15, 2020.

Stapen, C. (2014, January 29). Super Bowl Hotel Rates Drop Close to Game Day. *USA Today*.

Steeg, J. (1999, November 9). Inquiring Minds Should Know. *Fox Sports Biz Online*.

Su, R., & McDowell, E. (2020, February 2). How Super Bowl Ad Cost Have Skyrocketed Over the Years. *Business Insider*. https://www.businessinsider.com/super-bowl-ad-price-cost-2017-2.

Tampa Bay Super Bowl Host Committee. (2009). *FAQs*. http://tampabaysuperbowl.com/faqs.htm. Accessed December 1, 2009.

TNS Media Intelligence. (2009, February 11). TNS Media Intelligence Reports Academy Awards Spending Reached $691 Million. *TNS Media Intelligence online*. http://www.tns-mi.com/news/02112009.htm. Accessed November 30, 2009.

W.P. Carey Business School. (2008, April 23). *Economic Impact Study: Phoenix Scores Big with Super Bowl XLII*. https://news.wpcarey.asu.edu/20080423-economic-impact-study-phoenix-scores-big-super-bowl-xlii. Accessed August 29, 2020.

W.P. Carey Business School. (2015, July 22). *Super Bowl XLIX Delivered Super-Sized Returns*. https://news.wpcarey.asu.edu/20150722-super-bowl-xlix-delivered-super-sized-returns. Accessed July 31, 2020.

Young, J. (2019, December 30). With Football Ratings on the Rise, NFL Officials Look to Raise TV Broadcast Fees on Multiyear Media Deals. *CNBC*. https://www.cnbc.com/2019/12/30/nfl-ratings-recovering-new-media-deals-could-be-on-the-2020-agenda.html.

Zimbalist, A. (2015). *Circus Maximus: The Economic Gamble Behind Hosting the Olympics and the World Cup*. Washington, DC: Brookings Institution Press.

CHAPTER 4

The Players

Abstract The Super Bowl clearly makes teams and their players much happier. A championship can define the career of all the people involved. But what is the championship worth financially? We begin with the impact winning a Super Bowl has on a team's revenue. Because the NFL shares so much of its revenue, winning games doesn't seem to impact a team's earnings. But winning the Super Bowl does appear to have some value, although it is quite small. Our study of the players focuses primarily on the quarterbacks. We present evidence that winning a Super Bowl increases the pay of the winning quarterback. Perhaps surprisingly, the "best" quarterback doesn't seem to win the Super Bowl as often as one might think. Of course, it is possible identifying the "best" quarterback is not as clear as we might like!

Keywords Marginal Revenue Product · Revenue sharing · Fixed revenues · QB Score

The title game of the NFL has grown tremendously from its meager beginnings in 1932. Nearly 100 million people watched the Super Bowl in 2020 on television (Coster 2020). The game not only defines the best teams in the NFL, it has the power to define a player's career. Clearly the

Y. J. Kelly et al., *The Economics of the Super Bowl*, Palgrave Pivots in Sports Economics, https://doi.org/10.1007/978-3-030-46370-0_4

Super Bowl can make teams and players happy (or sad!). However, what is the financial impact of the Super Bowl on these players and teams?

From the team perspective we will look at how triumphing in the Super Bowl impacts team revenues. Our study of the player's perspective will be a bit more involved. Today we can't imagine anything preventing a player from performing on the game's biggest stage. We should note that historically that wasn't true. As reported by Klein (2019), in fact, in the first title game a star player was stopped by one college president. As bizarre as this sounds today, Dutch Clark hoped to play for the Portsmouth Spartans in the first title game in 1932. But because this game was not officially part of the schedule, Clark's boss—the president at Colorado College—wouldn't give his men's basketball coach permission to leave his "real" job to go play in a football game. So, Clark had to stay home.

Of course, given the meager state of the NFL in 1932, Clark didn't miss out on much. Certainly, that first championship game was nowhere near the spectacle that is the modern Super Bowl. Today, if something stopped Tom Brady or Patrick Mahomes from showing up…well, that would have to mean something, right?

This is the question we wish to answer. Specifically, we will look at how winning a Super Bowl impacts the financial fortunes of an NFL quarterback. In addition, we are going to look at how much quarterbacks today truly impact a team's fortunes both on and off the field.

To address these issues for the team and players requires we build three statistical models:

- A model of NFL revenue that will allow us to measure how much revenue a Super Bowl appearance and/or win has on team revenue.
- A model of quarterback salary that allows us to see how much teams pay a quarterback for playing in and/or winning the Super Bowl.
- A model of player productivity that will allow us to measure how many wins a quarterback produces and ultimately how important having a top quarterback is for a team's chances in the Super Bowl.

We tend to think the Super Bowl dramatically alters the fortunes of the teams and players involved with this spectacle. As we will see, the data seems inclined to tell a somewhat different story!

The Value of the Super Bowl to the Team

Here is the story one might tell about the Super Bowl. The teams on the field are not just competing for a championship that will make the coaches, players, and fans happy. The teams are also competing for a large financial prize. The winner of the Super Bowl will be rewarded with significantly more revenue in the future because everyone loves a winner. And the losers... well, they are going to get substantially less because they are losers!

Such a story reflects how we tend to think about sports. We tend to see sports as a meritocracy. The best teams win on the field. And the best teams also are rewarded the most financially.

Consider the story of the St. Louis Browns, a baseball franchise in the American League.[1] In the 52 seasons the Browns played baseball in St. Louis they only won more than they lost twelve times. And they only finished better than third in an eight-team American League three times. One of these times was in 1944 when many of the best baseball players were busy fighting World War II!

The inability of the Browns to win on the field was reflected in their attendance. In 1935 the average Major League Baseball team attracted nearly 6,300 fans per game.[2] The Browns—who only won 43% of their games that season—attracted less than 81,000 fans the entire season. In other words, this team barely averaged 1,000 fans per home game. Across their history in St. Louis, the Browns averaged less than 4,000 fans per home game. One might wonder how many people even noticed when this team left for Baltimore in 1953.

From a meritocracy perspective, the fate of the Browns seems deserved. The team was never very successful on the field and therefore it didn't deserve to see financial success. Of course, from the owners' perspective this was not a happy experience. Fifty years of struggles on the field and at the gate had to be a bit depressing.

Fortunately for sports owners today, the "sports as meritocracy" story has been changed. As Ourand (2020) reports, the NFL currently has several national broadcasting deals. The list includes...

[1] The history of the Browns performance on the field and home attendance can be found here: https://www.baseball-reference.com/teams/BAL/.

[2] Attendance in Major League Baseball in 1935 can be found here: https://www.baseball-reference.com/leagues/MLB/1935-misc.shtml.

- ESPN pays $1.9 billion per year for the right to broadcast "Monday Night Football."
- Fox and CBS both pay $1.1 billion per year for the right to broadcast games on Sunday afternoons.
- NBC pays $950 million per year to broadcast games on Sunday Night.
- Fox pays an additional $550 million per year for the rights to broadcast some games on Thursday nights.

Altogether, this works out to $5.6 billion per year for the NFL. And all of this is shared equally among all NFL teams. Whether your team appears frequently on national broadcasts or not, your team gets the same share of these billions.

As Howard Bloom (2014) notes, the NFL has been sharing its national television money equally among its teams since the early 1960s. But this is not the only revenue the league shares. Revenue from tickets and merchandise sales also tend to be shared. In all, Bloom (2014) reports that more than 60% of all revenue in the NFL is shared among its teams.

The exception to this story is the Dallas Cowboys. Bloom (2014) notes that America's Team (as the Cowboys are known at times) does not share any of their merchandise revenue with the other NFL teams. Bloom (2014) also reports that NFL teams don't share the revenue they get from sales of stadium suites, club seating, corporate sponsors, and naming rights. This also benefits the Cowboys. Their home, AT&T Stadium, has 342 suites that in 2014 were priced between $224,000 and $900,000 each.

The NFL's substantial revenue sharing program means the incentives for NFL teams are not quite what one might expect. As Berri (2015a) noted:

> ...although winning can make people in the NFL happier, the big economic story is that winning doesn't make owners in the NFL much richer. In sum, teams simply do not have much of a financial incentive to win. No matter what happens, next season there will be equal numbers of wins and losses across the league, because for every team that wins, another one loses. But not so for the owners: They, unlike their teams, will all get to be winners.

Perhaps nothing illustrates how the link between winning and revenue has been weakened in the NFL more than the 2008 Detroit Lions and the 2017 Cleveland Browns. Both of these teams finished these seasons with a 0–16 record. In other words, each of these teams did nothing but disappoint their customers for an entire season. One would think a business that offered nothing but sadness would be immensely unprofitable. But according to Forbes, both teams in their winless years had a positive operating income.

The experience of the winless Lions and Browns illustrates how little wins mean to a league that shares the majority of its revenue. We can see the same thing when we statistically measure the link between wins and revenue.

Our statistical model of revenue builds on the work of Berri et al. (2015). These authors argued that wins in professional sports are primarily a function of the following four measures: Wins, Market Size, Stadium Capacity, and Stadium Age. To this list we are going to add dummy variables to account for both winning and losing the Super Bowl.

Equation (1) illustrates this basic revenue model:

$$\begin{aligned}\text{Team Revenue} = a_{ik} &+ w_1 * \text{Wins} + a_2 * \text{Lagged Wins} \\ &+ a_3 * \text{Population} + a_4 * \text{Stadium Capacity} \\ &+ a_5 * \text{Stadium Age} + a_7 * \text{SBWin} + a_8 * \text{SBWinLag} \\ &+ a_9 * \text{SBLoss} + a_{10} * \text{SBLossLag} + e_t \qquad (1)\end{aligned}$$

where[3]

- Team Revenue = A team's total revenue as reported by Forbes[4]
- Wins = Wins in the current season
- Lagged Wins = Wins in the past season
- Population = Population in the Standard Metropolitan Statistical Area as reported by the Census Bureau in 2010[5]

[3] With the exception of stadium age, all of these factors would be expected to positively impact team revenue.

[4] Forbes reports this data yearly. It is accumulated at Rodney Fort's Sports Business Page (see https://sites.google.com/site/rodswebpages/codes).

[5] For Census data see https://www.census.gov/data/tables/time-series/demo/popest/2010s-total-metro-and-micro-statistical-areas.html.

- Stadium Capacity and Stadium Age can be found at the Stadiums of Pro Football website[6]
- SBWin = Dummy variable equal to one if a team won the Super Bowl
- SBWinLag = Dummy variable equal to one if a team won the Super Bowl last year
- SBLoss = Dummy variable equal to one if a team lost the Super Bowl
- SBLossLag = Dummy variable equal to one if a team lost the Super Bowl last year

Equation (1) was estimated across sixteen years of NFL data.[7] The results are reported in Table 4.1. What stands out from this exercise is the statistical insignificance of wins and lagged wins. It does not appear[8] additional wins cause a team's revenue to increase at all.[9] Market size also doesn't appear to matter. This explains why the NFL can place a franchise in Green Bay, Wisconsin; a place with a population barely above 100,000 people while also leaving the Los Angeles market, America's second largest metropolitan area with over 13 million residents, without a team for two decades at the beginning of the twenty-first century. This

[6] *Stadiums of Pro Football* (https://www.stadiumsofprofootball.com/comparisons/).

[7] Eq. (1) was estimated via the Prais-Winsten regression model. This was the same approach adopted by Berri et al. (2015). These authors built upon the work of Forrest and Simmons (2006), who examined demand for English League soccer. As Forest and Simmons (2006) noted: "An appropriate estimation method in our case is one which allows for the presence of AR(1) autocorrelation within panels plus cross-sectional correlation of errors and/or heterogeneity across panels. One such method is a Prais-Winsten regression model with panel corrected standard errors and common AR (1) autocorrelation parameter."

[8] It is important to emphasize the word "appears." Except for the Green Bay Packers (who are a public company), the NFL franchises do not have to report their financial information to the public. Our estimates of revenue come from Forbes. So, we are actually seeing how the factors in Eq. (1) relate to an estimate of team revenue. Statistical models should be interpreted with caution in general. In this case, perhaps a bit more caution is needed!

[9] Berri et al. (2015) looked at team revenue from 2002 to 2011. That study indicated that lagged wins was statistically insignificant but current wins were significant at the 10% level. As these authors noted, even if we argued that a 10% level of significance counts as "statistically significant," the size of the coefficient was immensely small. Again, this illustrated how little wins impacts team revenue in the NFL.

Table 4.1 Modeling NFL team revenue. Dependent variable: real total revenue[a]. Years: 2003–2018

Variable	*Coefficient*	*z-statistic*	*p-value*
Wins	$238,453	1.30	0.193
Wins, lagged	$103,847	0.56	0.574
Population in millions	$1,623,301	1.29	0.197
Stadium capacity*	$2905	4.53	0.000
Stadium age*	-$1,465,965	−5.77	0.000
Super Bowl win*	$6,968,802	3.05	0.002
Super Bowl win, last year*	$6,719,915	3.02	0.003
Super Bowl loss	$1,952,192	0.81	0.417
Super Bowl loss, last year	$2,282,023	1.08	0.282

*—denotes significance at the 1% level
[a]Revenue numbers from Forbes were converted into real 2019 dollars via the data on the Consumer Price Index reported by the Minneapolis Federal Reserve: https://www.minneapolisfed.org/community/financial-and-economic-education/cpi-calculator-information/consumer-price-index-and-inflation-rates-1913

result also explains how winless teams located in relatively small markets (i.e., Detroit and Cleveland) are still able to earn a profit. In a league where 60% of revenue is shared, one doesn't have to make a large number of people happy to survive.

We do see from this model that there is a small return to having a better stadium. The average NFL team across this sample earned more than $300 million in revenue. Each additional year a stadium ages costs a team less than $1.5 million. And increasing a stadium's capacity by 10,000 fans is worth less than $30 million. Relative to the revenues a team earns in a given year, the stadium effects—although statistically significant—seem relatively small. Of course, building a new stadium can still be worth money in a team's pockets, especially if the team can get the taxpayers to pay for the majority of the costs!

The same story can be told about the subject of our story. Winning the Super Bowl appears to have a statistically significant impact on revenue. But again, the size of the effect seems rather small. A Super Bowl victory increases revenue the current year by a bit less than $7 million. It also increases revenue the next year by a similar amount. Overall, though, the total effect is about \$13.4 million.[10] And losing the Super Bowl doesn't seem to be worth much of anything. Considering that our rough estimate of league-wide revenues from the Super Bowl that we calculated in the previous chapter works out to about \$20 million per team every year, even the teams that sit home every year during the Super Bowl, like the Detroit Lions, end up earning very similar amounts from the Super Bowl as do perennial Super Bowl contenders like the New England Patriots.

All of this tells a simple story about today's NFL. The NFL has managed to construct a sports league where competition determines winners on the field but keeps owners winning financially. In the end, coaches, players, and fans live and die with what happens in the game. Once again, though, no matter the final score the owners walk away victorious.

The Value of Winning the Super Bowl to the Quarterback

We have seen there is some evidence that winning the Super Bowl enriches the owners. We also know—from watching the Super Bowl—that winning this game apparently makes the players happier. But is there a financial benefit for the players?

Our focus here is going to be on the player most commonly called "The Face of the Franchise."[11] In the first 54 Super Bowls the winning quarterback (i.e., The Face of the Franchise) was named the game's Most Valuable Player 30 times. This is not surprising since quarterbacks are the only position that is credited with wins and losses in football. In addition, they are often the highest-paid players. In 2020 there are nine players whose average pay per year eclipses \$30 million.[12] All nine of these players are quarterbacks. If a player was going to benefit from winning a Super Bowl, we would expect it to be the quarterback.

[10] The impact of winning the Super Bowl two and three years ago was also considered. That effect was statistically insignificant.

[11] Berri et al. (2011) examined whether the attractiveness of the "face of the franchise" impacted a quarterback's pay. This study suggested that more attractive quarterbacks are paid more than less attractive quarterbacks. In other words, the phrase "face of the franchise" has a somewhat literal meaning.

[12] Source: https://www.spotrac.com/nfl/rankings/average/.

To see if this indeed happens all we need to do is build a salary model. Our approach is going to be based on the earlier work of Berri and Simmons (2009), Berri et al. (2011), and Berri (2019). Specifically, our dependent variable will be a measure of player compensation. Our list of independent variables will consider factors such as age, where a player was taken in the draft, and on-field performance. Of course, to this list we will consider whether or not a quarterback won the Super Bowl.

Player compensation in the NFL works a bit differently than in sports like basketball and baseball. In the NBA and Major League Baseball, contracts are guaranteed. This means once a player signs the contract, they will receive all the money in the deal regardless of their on-field performance (assuming they don't violate some clause in the contract). This means that player salary models in those sports generally focus on free agents because we expect the link between performance and salary to weaken the further a player is from the point the contract was signed.[13]

The NFL is different. Contracts in this league are not guaranteed. In essence, from the team's perspective every player is a free agent each season. Each year, teams walk away from deals they made with players in the past because the team no longer thinks the player is worth the value of the signed contract. And that means, if a team keeps a player it suggests they still think the player is worth the agreed upon money. As a consequence, Berri and Simmons (2009) and Berri et al. (2011) looked at the link between a quarterback's salary in a given season and that quarterback's performance the previous season. The year that the contract was officially signed was ignored.

The nature of NFL contracts also adds another wrinkle to our study of compensation. Berri (2019) offered a study of NBA free agent salaries and utilized average salary across the length of the contract as the measure of a player's compensation. Because these contracts in the NFL are not guaranteed, though, average salary across the contract could be misleading. A large salary on paper years into a deal may never been seen by a player who suffers from injury or age. Consequently, a better approach is to simply utilize what a player was paid that season as a measure of compensation.

But that choice is also not quite as clear as it appears. The NFL has a hard salary cap with a myriad of corresponding rules. The structure of

[13] In other words, we doubt the ability of decision-makers to truly forecast a player's performance several years into a contract. This is because injury and the effects of age are not perfectly predictable.

the cap often means what a player is paid in cash in a given season may not be the same as what the team is charged with respect to their cap. For example, teams often pay a signing bonus. Such a bonus is guaranteed to the player when they sign. But the bonus is charged to the cap across the length of the contract.[14] Therefore there is a difference between what a player costs in terms of the NFL salary cap in a given season and what is paid out in cash. For our purposes we are going to focus on the impact a quarterback had on a team's salary cap in a given season since it is the cap that is the binding constraint.[15]

Now that we have settled on the specific dependent variable in our salary model, let's talk about the independent variables (i.e., the factors we think explain pay). Following past research,[16] we begin with a quarterback's age and where they were selected in the draft. To this list we can consider whether or not a quarterback changed teams from the previous season and whether a quarterback is typically a starter or backup.

Then, there is performance on the field. There are many statistical measures one could consider. Pro Football Reference—our source for player statistics—reports more than 30 individual metrics to capture a quarterback's contribution as a passer and runner.[17] And those are just the statistics most football fans find familiar. There are also a host of

[14]For more on workings of the NFL Salary Cap see Fitzgerald (2013).

[15]A quarterback's impact on the salary cap can be found at the *Over the Cap* website. Data for 2020 can be found here: https://overthecap.com/position/quarterback/2020/.

Data for other years are also found at the same site. Compensation numbers were converted into real 2019 dollars via the data on the Consumer Price Index reported by the Minneapolis Federal Reserve: https://www.minneapolisfed.org/community/financial-and-economic-education/cpi-calculator-information/consumer-price-index-and-inflation-rates-1913.

This site does not report CPI data for 2020 so 2019 was taken to be the same as 2020.

[16]The list of factors we will consider begins with the work of Berri and Simmons (2009). In a study of salaries of NFL quarterbacks this work considered such factors as experience, career pass attempts, whether the quarterback was selected in the first or second round of the draft, market size, and whether or not the quarterback changed team. This study considers age instead of experience and will use team specific fixed effects instead of market size. It will also consider the difference between a quarterback selected in the top 10 picks of the draft and later in the first round.

[17]The career statistics of Matthew Stafford illustrates this abundance of statistics: https://www.pro-football-reference.com/players/S/StafMa00.htm.

"advanced" statistics that go beyond what you might see in a typical box score.

For our purposes we are going to focus on the most commonly noted measures. For example, the NFL's quarterback rating measure considers passing yards per attempt, touchdowns thrown per attempt, interceptions thrown per attempt, and completion percentage (i.e., completions per attempt). Beyond these four metrics, we will also consider total passing yards, rushing yards per rushing attempt, fumbles lost per play, and career pass attempts. This last factor is included as another effort to get at players who have more experience than others.

The final factors we will consider are related to team performance metrics. The first metric is fourth quarter comebacks during the previous season. Finally, we will consider Super Bowls won in a quarterback's career. All of these factors are listed in Eq. (2).

$$\begin{aligned}\text{Quarterback Pay} = a_{ik} &+ a_1 * \text{Age} + a_2 * \text{Age Squared} + a_3 * \text{Top10Pick} \\ &+ a_4 * \text{Late1stRound} + a_5 * \text{2ndRound} \\ &+ a_6 * \text{NewTeam} + a_7 * \text{CareerGSXP} + a_8 * \text{PassYds} \\ &+ a_9 * \text{PydsAtt} + a_{10} * \text{IntAtt} + a_{11} * \text{TDAtt} \\ &+ a_{12} * \text{CompPer} + a_{13} * \text{RushAvg} + a_{14} * \text{FumPlay} \\ &+ a_{15} * \text{CareerPatt} + a_{16} * \text{4thQCB} + a_{17} * \text{CareerSB}\end{aligned} \tag{2}$$

where[18]

- Age and Age Squared capture the effect we expect a quarterback's pay to initially increase as they age (due to the benefit of experience) and decline (due to the eventual impact of age)
- Top10Pick = dummy variable for quarterback taken with a top 10 pick in the annual NFL draft
- Late1stRound = dummy variable for quarterback taken in the first round of the draft, but outside the top 10 pick

[18] We would expect the following factors to have a positive impact on a quarterback's salary: Age, the factors associated with the draft, being a starter, the player statistics not related to turnovers, fourth quarter comebacks, and Super Bowls won. The other factors we would expect to have a negative impact.

- 2ndRound = dummy variable for quarterback taken in the second round
- NewTeam = dummy variable for quarterback who switches teams
- CareerGSXP = Number of games started in career per year of experience. This variable is designed to capture the difference between quarterbacks who generally start and those who do not
- PassYds = Passing yards the previous season
- PydsAtt = Passing yards per passing attempt the previous season
- IntAtt = Interceptions per passing attempt the previous season
- TDAtt = Touchdowns per passing attempt the previous season
- CompPer = Completion percentage the previous season
- RushAvg = Rushing Average the previous season
- FumPlay = Fumbles Lost per Play[19] the previous season
- CareerPatt = Career Pass Attempts
- 4thQCB = Number of fourth quarter comebacks the previous season
- CareerSB = Number of Super Bowl wins in career

The estimation of Eq. (2) is reported in Table 4.2. The results indicate that a quarterback's salary cap impact in a current season is statistically related to age (and age squared), being a top ten pick in the draft, changing teams, being a starter, passing yards, passing yards per attempt, fourth quarter comebacks, and Super Bowl wins. Pay does not appear to be related to being drafted outside the top ten or any other performance statistic.

The model estimated is a semi-logged model so the reported coefficients are not tremendously helpful. To get at how each of the statistically significant factors impact pay we multiply the reported coefficient by the average value of the dependent variable in the sample (the average quarterback has a real cap value of $9.36 million across the years considered).

Before we discuss the size of the estimated impacts, we should note something about the role of draft status and past quarterback performance. Consistent with Berri and Simmons (2009), there is some

[19] Fumbles lost is estimated as one-half of all fumbles. The number of plays is simply the summation of passing attempts, rushing attempts, and sacks.

Table 4.2 Modeling quarterback pay[a]. Dependent variable: Log of a quarterback's salary cap impact in 2019 dollars[b]. Years: 2013–2020. Team specific fixed effects employed

Variable	*Coefficient*	*z-statistic*	*p-value*
Age*	0.7383	4.69	0.000
Age squared*	−0.0114	−4.02	0.000
Top 10 pick***	0.2842	1.92	0.064
Last first round pick	−0.1386	−0.56	0.577
Second round pick	0.1931	0.78	0.442
New team**	−0.3484	−2.52	0.016
Career GS per year*	0.0529	2.59	0.014
Passing yards*	0.0002	2.83	0.008
Passing yards per attempt**	0.2822	2.46	0.019
Interceptions per attempt	−0.3383	−0.33	0.744
Touchdowns per attempt	0.8100	0.58	0.569
Completion percentage	0.3729	1.00	0.326
Rushing average	0.0179	0.48	0.636
Fumbles lost per play	−2.8281	−0.91	0.368
Career passing attempts	0.0001	0.90	0.377
Fourth quarter comebacks*	0.1001	2.76	0.009
Career Super Bowl wins**	0.2143	2.09	0.044
r^2	0.66		
Observations	376		

*—denotes significance at the 1% level
**—denotes significance at the 5% level
***—denotes significance at the 10% level
Robust standard errors were employed

[a]Like many salary models, this is a semi-logged model. The dependent variable is logged. The independent variables are not. Team specific fixed effects were employed

[b]Once again, salary numbers from Over the Cap were converted into real 2019 dollars via the data on the Consumer Price Index reported by the Minneapolis Federal Reserve: https://www.minneapolisfed.org/community/financial-and-economic-education/cpi-calculator-information/consumer-price-index-and-inflation-rates-1913

evidence that draft position impacts salary paid.[20] Such a result is consistent with the idea that quarterbacks taken earlier in the draft are better than those taken later. Berri and Simmons (2011), though, presented evidence that draft position doesn't tell us much about what a quarterback will do after the draft.

Table 4.3 updates this earlier work by looking at the correlation between where a quarterback was selected in the draft and their career performance the first eight years from the time they were drafted. As one can see, there is a correlation between where a quarterback is selected and how much they will play. Quarterbacks taken earlier do see the field more often. But when we look at performance per play, they are not getting more playing time because they are better quarterbacks.

The correlations (i.e., r) are instructive. But when we look at r^2—or the percentage of the variation in each factor that can be explained by where a quarterback is selected—we see clearly how little draft position relates to performance. In almost every case, less than 5% of the variation in a quarterback's performance can be explained by the slot where the quarterback was selected. In sum, predicting performance of a quarterback on draft day is really quite difficult. What is odd is that even after a team sees a quarterback play in the NFL, being a top ten pick still seems to impact pay.

A similar story can be told when we look at the performance of veteran quarterbacks. Table 4.4 reports the correlation between a quarterback's current performance and what that same quarterback did the previous season.[21]

As one can see, veteran quarterbacks are quite inconsistent. One can't explain more than 30% of a quarterback's current performance with their past performance in the same statistic.[22] The results are most stunning with respect to turnovers. A quarterback's propensity to commit turnovers

[20] In the specification reported, being selected with one of the top 10 picks in the draft is significant at the 10% level. If you leave out career pass attempts out of the model (a factor that is not significant), being a top 10 pick is significant at the 5% level.

[21] This point was originally made in Berri et al. (2006), Berri and Schmidt (2010), and Berri and Burke (2012).

[22] To put this in perspective, Berri and Schmidt (2010) report that in basketball 47% of a basketball player's field goal percentage is explained by what that player did the previous season. This is the lowest r^2 for any of the box score statistics in basketball. For rebounding, the year-to-year r^2 is 90%! In basketball, what you see in the previous season is generally what you get.

Table 4.3 Quarterback draft position and career performance. Relationship between where a quarterback is selected in the draft and career performance in the first eight years of a quarterback's career[a]. Minimum 100 plays per year[b]. Data from 1980 to 2019

	Year 1	*Year 2*	*Year 3*	*Year 4*	*Year 5*	*Year 6*	*Year 7*	*Year 8*
Correlations (r)								
Play per year	−0.490	−0.476	−0.437	−0.448	−0.482	−0.394	−0.410	−0.358
Passing yards per pass attempt	−0.217	−0.159	−0.119	−0.036	−0.116	−0.046	−0.113	−0.113
Touchdowns per pass attempt	−0.125	−0.060	−0.109	−0.001	−0.051	0.047	−0.049	−0.047
Interceptions per pass attempt	0.076	0.058	0.036	−0.110	0.003	0.003	0.004	−0.030
Completion percentage	−0.140	−0.076	−0.081	0.017	−0.178	−0.140	−0.164	−0.131
Rushing yards per rushing attempt	−0.119	−0.266	−0.197	−0.157	−0.182	−0.093	−0.122	−0.125
Fumbles lost per play	−0.001	−0.021	−0.054	−0.112	−0.053	−0.057	−0.037	−0.096
Explanatory power (r^2)								
Play per year	23.99%	22.67%	19.13%	20.05%	23.25%	15.50%	16.80%	12.81%
Passing yards per pass attempt	4.71%	2.51%	1.41%	0.13%	1.34%	0.21%	1.29%	1.28%
Touchdowns per pass attempt	1.57%	0.36%	1.18%	0.00%	0.26%	0.22%	0.24%	0.22%
Interceptions per pass attempt	0.58%	0.34%	0.13%	1.22%	0.00%	0.00%	0.00%	0.09%
Completion percentage	1.96%	0.58%	0.65%	0.03%	3.16%	1.96%	2.69%	1.72%
Rushing yards per rushing attempt	1.42%	7.09%	3.86%	2.47%	3.30%	0.86%	1.49%	1.56%
Fumbles lost per play	0.00%	0.04%	0.29%	1.25%	0.28%	0.32%	0.14%	0.92%

[a]Performance data and draft information can be found at Pro-Football-Reference.com

[b]This means a quarterback in year seven needed to have 700 plays at that point to be included in the study

Table 4.4 Veteran quarterback performance. Correlation in veteran quarterback performance[a]. Minimum 100 pass attempts. Season: 2000–2019

Performance statistic	*Correlation (r)*	r^2
Passing yards per attempt	0.40	0.16
Touchdowns per attempt	0.30	0.09
Completion percentage	0.54	0.29
Interceptions per passing attempt	0.20	0.04
Fumbles per play	0.20	0.04

[a]Performance data found at Pro-Football-Reference.com

is essentially random. In other words, when announcers in an NFL broadcast chide a quarterback for throwing an interception or fumbling the ball… well, those comments appear to be nonsense. Turnovers are not something quarterbacks can easily control. Hence, we should not be surprised that neither interceptions or fumbles impact a quarterback's pay (i.e., teams seem to know this!).

The stories told by Tables 4.3 and 4.4 should not be surprising. Unlike sports like baseball and basketball,[23] a football player's performance depends tremendously on the play of their teammates. A quarterback completing a pass requires a receiver to catch the ball, an offensive line to block, and a coach to call the right play. Change the people (or their performance) around the quarterback and you are likely to change the results observed.

Although NFL decision-makers do not appear to be influenced by turnovers, it does appear passing yards per attempt do impact how much money they are willing to allocate to the quarterback position. How much are they willing to pay for this relatively unreliable statistic?

Table 4.5 reports the economic impact of the statistically significant factors from Table 4.2.[24] For passing yards per attempt we consider how a one standard deviation change in this statistic impacts compensation. As one can see, such an improvement is worth a bit less than $2 million. A

[23]Basketball players are the most consistent players in the major North American sports (i.e., baseball, basketball, hockey, and football). Although it appears a player depends on her/his teammates in basketball, that is generally not true. Great players in basketball tend to be great no matter where they are employed and there is not much one can do to change the performance of poor players. For more on this, see Berri and Schmidt (2010).

[24]The one factor left out of Table 4.5 is age. Both age and age squared are significant. The estimated results indicate that quarterback pay peaks at 32.2 years of age. Other specifications indicated that this peak was closer to 30.

Table 4.5 Economics factors impacting quarterback pay. The Economic impact of the factors statistically impacting quarterback pay

Performance statistic	*Economic impact*
... a one standard deviation change	
Games started per year*	$2,588,849
Passing yards*	$2,795,315
Passing yards per attempt**	$1,951,823
... a one-unit increase	
New team**	−$3,259,707
Top 10 pick**	$2,658,807
Career Super Bowl wins**	$2,005,315
Fourth quarter comebacks**	$936,137

similar approach was taken to games started and passing yards. Both of those factors have a larger impact on player pay.

Table 4.5 also reports the economic impact of changing teams, fourth quarter comebacks, and Super Bowl victories. Of these, we are most interested in the latter. Our model indicates that winning a Super Bowl increases a quarterback's compensation by about $2 million. Again, we learned earlier that winning a Super Bowl is worth $13.4 million in revenue to a team. Putting these results together suggests that teams give a substantial portion of the gain to winning the Super Bowl to the winning quarterback.[25]

It should be noted that the model was also estimated with simple dummy variables for winning the Super Bowl in the current season or past seasons. The simple dummies were not generally significant. Career Super Bowls won, though, was generally significant in a variety of specifications (although not all!). Given the sample we are considering, this result might be driven a great deal by just Tom Brady (who has won 6 Super Bowls in the twenty-first century)! In sum, the reported results are sensitive to how the model is specified which should be kept in mind in interpreting these results.

[25] The return on the Super Bowl for the team is across two years. Career Super Bowls won impacts a quarterback's pay going forward. So, the return to the quarterback over time is more than $2 million.

Is Tom Brady the Best? Depends on Your Universe!

Table 4.5 suggests teams think quarterbacks have a very large impact on a team's Super Bowl chance. But is this accurate? It certainly seems to defy a story coaches often tell.

Coaches often preach in team sports that everyone on the team matters. The team wins together and it loses together. No one player is more important than any other. Although this is a story coaches often tell, it is clear some players are more important than others. For example, pitchers in baseball are credited with "wins" and "losses." Apparently, just like in George Orwell's Animal Farm, all of the players are equal, but some are more equal than others.

This practice doesn't seem to make much sense. Pitchers are primarily defensive players. Although pitchers do bat in the National League, no team is pinning their hopes for victories on the offensive prowess of the pitchers who do get to hit. Clearly a team needs offense to win a game. Therefore, it doesn't make much sense to credit the outcome of the game on a player who only really makes a contribution to one half of the contest.

Of course—as noted—a similar story can be told about football. Quarterback Tom Brady started 324 regular season games with the New England Patriots from 2001 to 2019. Across these games, the Patriots won 249 times. Therefore—according to NFL convention—Brady "won" 249 games; a mark that ranks first in NFL history.[26]

A similar story can be told about the NFL postseason. Brady started 41 playoff games for the Patriots. The Patriots managed to win 30 of these games. Again, these wins are credited to Brady and therefore Brady also ranks first in NFL history in postseason wins.[27]

Six of these wins came in the Super Bowl. No one in NFL history has won more Super Bowls than Brady. And that must mean Brady is the greatest winner ever to play football. Right?

Well, maybe not.

In Super Bowl LI (i.e., Super Bowl 51), Brady and the Patriots faced Matt Ryan and the Atlanta Falcons. As detailed in Berri (2017a), with less

[26] Source: https://www.footballdb.com/stats/qb-records.html?type=&alltime=1&sort=w.

[27] Source: https://www.footballdb.com/stats/qb-records.html?alltime=1&type=post&letter=&sort=w.

than five minutes remaining in the contest the Falcons were ahead 28-20. The Falcons also had a first down with the ball on the Patriots' 22-yard line. From that range, the Falcons' field goal kicker had only missed once all year. That means Atlanta could have sat on the ball for three plays and just kicked a field goal. Brady and the Patriots would have gotten the ball back, but would have needed to score twice in a very short period of time to avoid losing.

Unfortunately for Atlanta fans, Kyle Shanahan—the offensive coordinator for the Falcons—decided not to sit on the ball. After losing one yard on a first-down run, Shanahan decided to pass the ball. Over the next three plays the Falcons suffered a sack, an offensive line penalty, and an incomplete pass. All of that pushed the Falcons completely out of field goal range. After a punt back to the Patriots, Tom Brady led his team for a touchdown and a successful two-point conversion. In overtime, Brady and the Patriots scored again to win the Super Bowl.[28]

Two years earlier a similar scenario played itself out. In Super Bowl XLIX (i.e., Super Bowl 49) Tom Brady and the Patriots faced Russell Wilson and the Seattle Seahawks. With a bit more than two minutes left in the game the Patriots were up 28-24. Wilson, though, quickly drove the Seahawks down the field. With a bit more than a minute left Seattle had a first down on the Patriots five-yard line. Seattle then elected to run the ball and Marshawn Lynch—the team's Pro Bowl running back—moved the ball to the one-yard line. Now it was second down with 26 seconds left. All the Seahawks needed was one yard to win the Super Bowl! Most everyone assumed the ball would go back to Lynch. He had already rushed for 100 yards that day. But Seattle decided to pass the ball. Unfortunately, the pass was intercepted and once again Brady and the Patriots were Super Bowl champs.

Berri (2017a) asks us to imagine life for Brady if things had gone slightly differently:

> …imagine a parallel universe. In this one the Seahawks choose to give the ball to Lynch and he scores the winning touchdown. If that happens, Brady is not a hero. In fact, if Seattle and Atlanta both made different choices we would be living in a parallel universe where a very different story would be told about Brady. We would now be wondering how a

[28] Shanahan left the Falcons a day after this Super Bowl and became head coach of the San Francisco 49ers.

> quarterback who won three Super Bowls when he was younger suddenly became a quarterback who lost four Super Bowls across 12 seasons.

Before Brady and the Patriots defeated Seattle in Super Bowl XLIX, the Patriots hadn't won a Super Bowl in ten years. And if we looked back at the three Super Bowls Brady had won before Super Bowl XLIX, we may not be impressed. In all three victories Brady and the Patriots had only won by a single field goal.

Had the Falcons and Seahawks simply run the ball, it is very possible that in 2017 people would be wondering whatever happened to Tom Brady. How did a player who won three Super Bowls in his younger days suddenly start losing every time he got his team to the biggest stage? And those questions would have been even louder when the Patriots lost Super Bowl LII (i.e., Super Bowl 52) to the Philadelphia Eagles. In the aforementioned parallel universe (where Brady's opponents remember to run the ball), Brady would have been a loser in five consecutive Super Bowl appearances.

As Berri (2017a) argues:

> It is important to emphasize that this parallel universe is not created by the choices Brady made. This parallel universe was created by different choices made the opposing team's offenses in the Super Bowl. Because these other teams chose poorly, Brady has morphed from an older quarterback who can't win anymore into a quarterback that many consider the greatest ever. In both universes, Brady is the same player. But in one universe (the one you and I live in) Brady played opponents who apparently didn't make great choices. And in the parallel universe, Brady's opponents were slightly smarter.

The story of Tom Brady and parallel universes emphasizes an important point about how we evaluate quarterbacks. History is obviously written backwards. We look at the outcome and then construct a story of how we got there. When we do that with respect to Tom Brady, the story we tell is that Brady is football's greatest winner. But we can't look at team outcomes and think that tells us about the contribution of an individual player. To understand the contribution of Tom Brady and any other quarterback, we have to make some effort to separate a quarterback's productivity from the productivity of his teammates. In sum, what we need to do is understand player statistics.

Who Are the Best Quarterbacks?

In 1970, Don Smith led a committee employed by the NFL to create a single metric that would summarize much of what a quarterback does in a single number. The number—called the Quarterback Rating by the NFL—involves the following very convoluted steps[29]:

> First one takes a quarterback's completion percentage, then subtracts 0.3 from this number and divides by 0.2. You then take yards per attempts, subtract 3 and divide by 4. After that, you divide touchdowns per attempt by .05. For interceptions per attempt, you start with .095, subtract from this number interceptions per attempt, and then divided this result by .04. To get the quarterback rating, you add the values created from your first four steps, multiply this sum by 100, and divide the result by 6. Oh, and by the way, the sum from each of your first four steps cannot exceed 2.375 or be less than zero.

As described by Berri and Burke (2012), there is some sense to all of this. Essentially what Smith and his team were trying to do is normalize four statistics—completion percentage (completions divided by pass attempts), yards per pass attempt, touchdowns per pass attempt, and interceptions per attempt—around the averages that existed in 1970. So, although it appears nonsensical, some thought went into this metric.

It remains the case today that NFL broadcasts still report the Quarterback Rating for the passers in each game. Despite the fact this is still used today, it is clear this isn't a particularly good measure of a quarterback's contribution to team success. To begin with, the measure completely ignores everything a quarterback does with his feet. This measure also ignores fumbles. There is also no attempt to measure how each statistic impacts wins. And finally—if that wasn't enough—comparing a passer today to the averages that existed in 1970 is a very bad idea. The best quarterback in 1970 according to the Quarterback Rating was John Brodie.[30] His mark of 93.8 would rank 13th in the NFL in 2019. Brodie also led all passers in 1970 with 210.1 passing yards per game. In 2019 that mark would have ranked 27th in the league. In sum, the top passer

[29] Berri and Burke (2012).

[30] https://www.pro-football-reference.com/years/1970/passing.htm. https://www.pro-football-reference.com/years/2019/passing.htm.

in 1970 might have had trouble keeping his job with those numbers in 2019!

Fortunately, we can do a bit better than this metric. In Berri et al. (2006), Berri (2007), and Berri and Burke (2012) an alternative measure was offered that solves many of the issues with the NFL's favorite quarterback measure. In essence this model does what we commonly see in baseball and basketball. Specifically, if you wish to know the value of statistics tracked for players one simply builds a statistical model that connects those player statistics to team outcomes.[31]

Our objective in building such a model is to ascertain a value—in terms of wins—of the statistics commonly tracked for a quarterback. Such a model can answer

- how many wins does each additional passing or rushing yard create?
- how many wins are lost when a quarterback throws an incomplete pass?
- how many wins are lost when a quarterback throws an interception or loses a fumble?

The answers to these questions require that we answer a bigger question: What determines a team's ability to win?

To answer this question, we first turn to the work of Bill Gerrard (2007). As noted by Gerrard (2007), American football—like soccer (i.e., real football!), basketball, and hockey—is a "complex invasion sport." Gerrard (2007) describes such sports as follows:

> Invasion team sports involve a group of players co-operating to move an object (e.g. a ball or puck) to a particular location defended by opponents (e.g. across a line or between goalposts). There are several dimensions of complexity in invasion team sports. First the range of player actions is much greater and includes tackling to regain possession, moving the ball forward via passing, receiving, running and/or dribbling, and attempting to score

[31] Specifically, one employs a regression—or series of regressions—in creating a measure of individual player performance. The work of Asher Blass (1992)—which builds on earlier Sabermetric work—is a good example of how to evaluate hitters with a regression model. Voros McCracken (2001) offered a regression to better evaluate pitchers. Berri et al. (2006), Berri (2008), and Berri and Schmidt (2010) offers a measure of basketball productivity based on regression analysis.

by shooting or crossing the line. Second player actions are highly independent. Scoring requires the ball to be moved forward which in turn requires the team to have regained possession. Defensive and offensive plays are interdependent. Third, many player actions are joint actions. For example, more than one player may join together to tackle an opponent in possession in some codes of football. Fourth, invasion games vary in the degree to which there is continuity or segmentation between offensive and defensive plays. Association football (i.e. soccer) is the most complex in this respect with a continuous flow whereas American football is highly segmented with play stopped and players interchanged after turnovers in possession. Finally, linked to the degree of continuity in play, invasion games vary in the extent to which playing roles are specialised. Again soccer is the most complex in this respect with all outfield players required to be highly competent both defensively and offensively. In contrast American football has highly specialised defensive, offensive and kicking units.

As Gerrard (2007) argues, although these sports might appear to be different, complex invasion sports can generally be captured by a collection of structural equations similar to what Gerrard offers to describe soccer:

(SE1) League Points = f(Goals Scored, Goals Conceded)
(SE2) Goals Scored = Own Conversion Rate × Own Shots At Goal
(SE3) Goals Conceded = (1 − Own Save-Shot Ratio) × Opposition Shots On Target
(SE4) Own Shots At Goal = f(Own General Play)
(SE5) Opposition Shots On Target = f(Own General Play)

where general play includes number of passes, pass completion rate, crosses, dribbles, tackles won, interceptions, blocks and clearances. (Source: Gerrard [2007])

The model employed by Berri (2008) to measure player productivity in basketball follows the approach offered by Gerrard (2007).[32] As Berri and Burke (2012) notes, applying the Gerrard (2007) approach to American football involves estimating three basic relationships.

The process of applying this approach to the NFL begins with the most obvious relationship. Wins in the NFL are clearly a function of points

[32] The model form Berri (2008) was originally presented in Berri et al. (2006). In essence, Gerrard (2007) and Berri (2008) came independently to the same conclusion about how to model a sport.

Table 4.6 Modeling wins in the NFL. Dependent variable: team winning percentage. Years: 2011–2019. Team and year fixed effects were employed

Variable	Label	Coefficient	t-statistic	p-value
Points for per game	PFgm*	0.0264	26.49	0.000
Points against per game	PAgm*	−0.0309	−16.84	0.000
r^2	0.84			
Observations	288			

Note The data utilized to estimate this model came from https://www.pro-football-reference.com/
Robust standard errors were employed
*—denotes significance at the 1% level

scored and points surrendered. As Table 4.6 illustrates, 84% of a team's winning percentage[33] is explained by how many points a team scores and surrenders per game in a season. This model indicates that a team that scores five more points per game will see their winning percentage increase by 0.132. That is 2.1 additional wins across a sixteen-game season.

The next step is to determine what factors explain how many points a team scores and surrenders in a season. Once again, we are primarily interested in how the statistics tracked for the quarterback related to points scored and points surrendered. To ascertain the impact of the quarterbacks' statistics, though, we need to consider all the other factors that impact scoring.

As Table 4.7 illustrates, the factors that impact the ability of a team's offense to score can be divided into three categories. First a team must acquire the ball. This is captured by considering all of a team's drives that did not begin with a turnover, the opponent's interceptions, and the opponent's fumbles lost.[34]

[33] Occasionally an NFL games ends in a tie. When that happens, a team's wins were increased by 0.5.

[34] In Berri and Burke (2012) it was noted a team acquires the ball via the opponent's turnovers (i.e., interceptions and fumbles lost), opponent's failed fourth down conversions, opponent's missed field goals, opponent's punts, and opponent's kickoffs. The football data utilized for this book came from https://www.pro-football-reference.com/ and this site does not seem to report how many times each team's opponent kicked off. Our study of quarterbacks requires we see how turnovers impact outcomes. But the other methods of acquiring the ball do not need to be separated out to evaluate quarterbacks. Consequently, DriveNonTOV was constructed as a replacement for these non-turnover factors. This is simply the number of drives a team has minus the opponent's turnovers.

Table 4.7 Factors impacting the ability of a team's offense to score. Expected impact of each factor (+ or −) reported after each variable

Actions	*Variables tabulated*
Acquisition of the ball	Number of drives not started by an opponent turnover (DRIVEnonTOV) (+)
	Opponent's interceptions (Opp.INT) (+)
	Opponent's fumbles lost (Opp.FUMLOST) (+)
Moving the ball	Average starting position of drives (START) (+)
	Total offensive yards gained = OFFYDS = RUSHYDS + PASSYDS (+)
	Total rushing yards gained (RUSHYDS)
	Total passing yards gained (PASSYDS)
	Net penalty yards (NETPENYDS) = Penalty yard − Opponent's penalty yards (−)
Maintaining possession	PLAYS = RUSHATT + PASSATT + SACKED (−)
	Rushing attempts (RUSHATT)
	Passing attempts (PASSATT)
	Sacks (SACKED)
	Interceptions (INT) (−)
	Fumbles lost (FUMLOST) (−)
	Failed fourth down conversion (4THFAIL) (−)
	Missed field goals (FGMISS) (−)
	Punts (PUNTS) (−)

Once the team has the ball it must move the ball across the field. The ability of a team to do this is captured by the average starting position of its drives, how many yards the team gains on offense, and both the team's and its opponent's penalties (this is captured with net penalty yards). Of these factors we are most interested in the value associated with its offensive yards (i.e., passing and rushing yards).

A team doesn't just need to move the ball. It also has to keep the ball. The ability to maintain possession is captured by how many plays the team has, its own turnovers, its failures on 4th down, missed field goals, and its punts.

All of this is summarized with Eq. (3).

$$
\begin{aligned}
\text{Offensive Scoring} = a_{ik} &+ a_1 * \text{DriveNonTO} + a_2 * \text{Opp.INT} \\
&+ a_3 * \text{Opp.FUMLOST} + a_4 * \text{START} \\
&+ a_5 * \text{OFFYDS} + a_6 * \text{NetPenYds} \\
&+ a_7 * \text{PLAYS} + a_8 * \text{INT}
\end{aligned}
$$

Table 4.8 Modeling offensive scoring. Dependent variable: scoring by a team's offense. Years: 2011–2019. Team and year fixed effects were employed

Variable	*Label*	*Coefficient*	*t-statistic*	*p-value*
Drives (not started by opponent turnovers)	DrivesNonTO*	2.206	9.96	0.000
Opponent's interceptions thrown	Opp.INT**	2.334	8.95	0.000
Opponent's fumbles lost	Opp.FUMLOST*	3.290	11.22	0.000
Average starting position of drives	START*	3.909	6.03	0.000
Yards gained, offense	OFFYDS*	0.048	15.18	0.000
Net penalty yards	NETPEN**	−0.016	−2.57	0.015
Plays	PLAYS*	−0.092	−3.08	0.004
Interceptions thrown	INT*	−2.611	−10.21	0.000
Fumbles lost	FUMLOST*	−2.124	−6.92	0.000
Failed 4th down conversion	4THFAIL*	−1.894	−5.71	0.000
Field goals missed	FGMISS*	−3.558	−8.64	0.000
Punts	PUNTS*	−2.315	−12.24	0.000
r^2	0.93			
Observations	288			

Note The data utilized to estimate this model came from https://www.pro-football-reference.com/
Robust standard errors were employed
*—denotes significance at the 1% level
**—denotes significance at the 5% level
***—denotes significance at the 10% level

$$+ a_9 * \text{FUMLOST} + a_{10} * \text{4thFAIL} \\ + a_{11} * \text{FGMISS} + a_{12} * \text{PUNTS} \quad (3)$$

The estimation of Eq. (3) is reported in Table 4.8. As one can see, these factors explain[35] 93% of the variation of the scoring by a team's

[35] Berri and Burke (2012) also considered how a team scores. This was captured with touchdown percentage, or the percentage of a team's offensive scores that were touchdowns [(Passing TD + Rushing TD)/(Passing TD + Rushing TD + Field Goals Made)]. One could also capture a similar effect with a team's Red Zone Percentage (i.e., Red Zone Touchdowns/Red Zone Attempts or RZper) or percentage of times a team scores a touchdown once they cross the opponent's 20-yard line (i.e., the Red Zone). If we add Red Zone Percentage to this model, explanatory power increases to 96%. One could argue, though, that because Red Zone Percentage is a scoring factor, one might be trying to explain a team's ability to score with a metric that captures a team's ability to score. The

offense.[36] All of the independent variables also have the expected sign, and except for Net Penalty Yards, all coefficients are significant at the 1% level.

Quarterbacks only play on offense so one might think we can stop with our model of offensive scoring. Unfortunately, what a quarterback does can also impact his defense. Specifically, turnovers by the quarterback also make it more likely the opponent will score. To capture this effect, we also need a model of a team's defense.

Fortunately, such a model is quite easy to construct. As noted in Berri (2007), such a model simply requires we reverse the independent variables listed in Eq. (2). For example, instead of using yards gained by a team's offense (OFFYDS), we now employ the yards gained by the opponent's offense (Opp.OFFYDS). The other factors listed in Eq. (3) were chosen by the same process.[37]

$$
\begin{aligned}
\text{Opponent's Offensive Scoring} = a_{ik} &+ a_1 * \text{Opp.DriveNonTO} + a_2 * \text{INT} \\
&+ a_3 * \text{FUMLOST} + a_4 * \text{Opp.START} \\
&+ a_5 * \text{Opp.OFFYDS} + a_6 * \text{NetPenYds} \\
&+ a_7 * \text{Opp.PLAYS} + a_8 * \text{Opp.INT} \\
&+ a_9 * \text{Opp.FUMLOST} \\
&+ a_{10} * \text{Opp.4THFAIL} \\
&+ a_{11} * \text{Opp.FGMISS} \\
&+ a_{12} * \text{Opp.PUNTS}
\end{aligned}
\qquad (4)
$$

The estimation of Eq. (4) is reported in Table 4.9. As one can see, 89% of the variation in the scoring by the opponent's offense[38] can

results of interest (i.e., what we learn about quarterbacks) is essentially the same whether Red Zone Percentage is included or not. Consequently, this factor was dropped from the model.

[36]The dependent variable in this model is not all of the points a team scores. Some scoring is done by a team's defense. In addition, extra points follow every touchdown whether it is scored by the offense or defense. To get at the proficiency of a team's offense, only scoring directly linked to a team's offense is considered. Consequently, points scored by the offense only considers points from passing touchdowns, points from rushing touchdowns, and field goals made.

[37]The lone exception is Net Penalty Yards. This is defined the same in both Eqs. (2) and (3).

[38]Again, this is just scoring attributed to an opponent's offense. So, this includes the opponent's passing touchdowns, rushing touchdowns, and field goals.

Table 4.9 Modeling opponent's scoring. Dependent variable: opponent's offensive points for (Opp. OffPF). Years: 2011–2019. Team and year fixed effects were employed

Variable	*Label*	*Coefficient*	*t-statistic*	*p-value*
Opponent's Drives (not started by opponent turnovers)	DrivesNonTO*	2.1127	9.55	0.000
Interceptions thrown	INT*	2.5417	9.53	0.000
Fumbles lost	FUMLOST*	2.7726	7.56	0.000
Opponent average starting position of drives	Opp.START*	3.7430	5.87	0.000
Opponent YARDS GAINED, OFFENSE	Opp.OFFYARDS*	0.0437	10.86	0.000
Net penalty yards	NETPEN*	0.0201	3.43	0.001
Opponent's plays	Opp.PLAYS*	−0.0832	−2.67	0.008
Opponent's interceptions thrown	Opp. INT*	−2.7416	−11.56	0.000
Opponent's fumbles lost	Opp. FUMLOST*	−2.0859	−6.66	0.000
Opponent's failed 4th down conversion	Opp.4THFAIL*	−2.2006	−6.71	0.000
Opponent's field goals missed	Opp.FGMISS*	−3.0512	−8.18	0.000
Opponent's punts	Opp. PUNTS*	−2.2210	−9.83	0.000
r^2	0.89			
Observations	288			

Note The data utilized to estimate this model came from https://www.pro-football-reference.com/
Robust standard errors were employed
*—denotes significance at the 1% level

be explained by the independent variables employed. And each of the estimated coefficients is statistically significant at the 1% level.

As we have noted, we are primarily interested in the factors associated with the quarterback. These include yards attributed to the quarterback (rushing yards, passing yards, and sack yards), plays attributed to the quarterback (rushing attempts, passing attempts, and sacks) and turnovers (interceptions and fumbles lost). Looking back at Tables 4.8 and 4.9, we can now ascertain the impact of all these statistics on both a team's point differential (points for minus points against) and wins. This is reported in Table 4.10.

As one can see, turnovers have a very large impact on outcomes. In general, an interception thrown both costs a team about 2.6 points on

Table 4.10 Marginal value of various quarterback statistics. NFL team data: 2011–2019

Variable	*Impact on point differential of a one unit increase in*	*Impact on wins of a one unit increase in*
Yards (rushing yards, passing yards, and sack yards)	0.0485	0.0013
Plays (rushing attempts, passing attempts, and sacks)	−0.0918	−0.0024
Interceptions	−5.1531	−0.1474
Fumbles lost	−4.8970	−0.1417

offense and adds about 2.5 points to an opponent's scoring. So, the net impact is over five points. A similar story is told about fumbles lost. If we look at the value of a yard, a quarterback would need to accumulate more than 100 yards to offset the negative impact of a turnover.[39]

The results from Table 4.10 allow us to estimate how many net points and wins each quarterback produces. To do this one simply multiplies the marginal values listed in Table 4.10 by each quarterback's accumulation of the corresponding statistic.[40] Table 4.11 reports this calculation for Patrick Mahomes in 2019.

As one can see, Mahomes accumulation of yards was worth 5.3 wins. But when we consider his plays and turnovers, his overall value was 3.0 wins. As Table 4.12 notes, that production led all quarterbacks in 2019.

One of the issues with the NFL's metric is that it seems immensely convoluted.[41] The calculation of Net Points and Wins Produced is quite

[39] This result is different from what was reported in Berri and Burke (2012). That model was estimated with data from 1995 to 2010. In addition to a different time period, the models for offensive and defensive scoring are somewhat different here. As noted, instead of including all the way a team acquires the ball the models here only look at number of drives and turnovers. This change, though, resulted in very similar estimates. In other words, the results from 2011 to 2019 were almost identical to what was seen from 1995 to 2009. At least, that was the case until one more change was made. That change was replacing Third Down Conversion Rate (utilized in the early work) with the number of punts. That change—by itself—increased the explanatory power of the models and essentially doubled the impact of turnovers on outcomes.

[40] Often only fumbles are reported for a quarterback. We are interested in actual turnovers. To estimate fumbles lost one simply takes half of the reported fumbles.

[41] The measure developed here improves upon the NFL's measure by considering sacks (and yards lost from sacks), rushing attempts (and yards gained from rushing) and fumbles.

Table 4.11 The value of Patrick Mahomes in 2019

Statistic	*Marginal value*	*Totals*	*Wins produced*
All Yards (passing yards, rushing yards, sack yards)	0.0013	4122	5.3
All Plays (passing attempts, rushing attempts, sacks)	−0.0024	544	−1.3
Interceptions	−0.1474	5	−0.7
Fumbles lost (estimated)	−0.1417	1.5	−0.2
		Total	3.0

Table 4.12 The top quarterbacks in 2019

Rank	*Player*	*Net points*	*Wins produced*
1	Patrick Mahomes	116.7	3.00
2	Dak Prescott	110.7	2.75
3	Aaron Rodgers	98.9	2.53
4	Russell Wilson	96.3	2.43
5	Lamar Jackson	96.8	2.43
6	Drew Brees	82.6	2.13
7	Derek Carr	80.9	2.00
8	Tom Brady	77.1	1.92
9	Kirk Cousins	66.1	1.61
10	Carson Wentz	56.3	1.30
11	Ryan Tannehill	52.9	1.29
12	Kyler Murray	55.0	1.28
13	Matthew Stafford	49.4	1.21
14	Gardner Minshew II	51.2	1.20
15	Jacoby Brissett	49.2	1.18
16	Deshaun Watson	50.9	1.14
17	Matt Ryan	50.0	1.10
18	Jared Goff	49.0	1.04
19	Jimmy Garoppolo	41.6	0.88
20	Teddy Bridgewater	29.8	0.76

But it leaves out touchdowns. Obviously one can explain 100% of scoring by considering scoring. So, a regression designed to explain scoring can't include touchdowns (or scoring measures) as an explanatory variable. One should note, any measure for a quarterback that directly includes touchdowns will explains wins better than a measure that doesn't. Scoring does explain wins. Our objective here is to understand how quarterbacks impact scoring.

a bit easier. We can, though, do even better. As was done originally in Berri et al. (2006), the results reported in Table 4.10 can be simplified. As one can see, the marginal impact of a play—in absolute terms—is about twice the impact of one additional yard. In addition—as already noted—the marginal impact of one turnover is similar to the impact of 100 yards. Given this, QB Score would be calculated as follows.[42]

$$\text{QB Score} = \text{All Yards} - 2 * \text{All Plays} \quad - \quad 100 * \text{All Turnovers}$$

If we look at a sample of quarterbacks with a minimum of 100 pass attempts in a season from 1970 to 2019 (2028 observations) we see a 0.99 correlation between QB Score per play and Wins per 100 plays. In essence, one can evaluate quarterbacks with the simple QB Score metric and essentially achieve the same ranking as one sees when one measures how many wins a quarterback produces.

This is illustrated in Table 4.13 where the top 20 quarterbacks in QB Score for 2019 is reported. As one can see, 19 of the 20 quarterbacks listed in Table 4.13 are the same as those listed in Table 4.12.[43]

Both Tables 4.12 and 4.13 tell us that Patrick Mahomes was the best quarterback in 2019. In the Super Bowl, his team was opposed by Jimmy Garoppolo who was ranked 19th in both tables. When the Super Bowl was over, Mahomes and his team prevailed. Yes, in 2019 the best quarterback led his team to the title, but how often does this actually happen in the NFL?

If we are simply going to say quarterbacks score by themselves, we might as well just claim quarterbacks also win by themselves.

[42] In Berri and Burke (2012), QB Score had this formulation:

$$\text{QB Score} = \text{All Yards} - 2 * \text{All Plays} \quad - \quad 100 * \text{All Turnovers}$$

Again, that is what you see if you employ third down conversion rate instead of punts.

[43] Quarterbacks do not all appear on the field with the same frequency. Therefore it is often useful to compare quarterbacks per play. Such a comparison also requires a sense of what an average quarterback does. In 2019, the average quarterback posted a 1.41 QB Score and 0.067 Net Points per play. Wins Produced are quite small per play so for that statistic it is useful to calculate Wins Produced per 100 plays (WP100). The average quarterback in 2019 posted a 0.145 WP100. As you go back in time you see quarterbacks did much less and each of those numbers tends to be smaller. So the "best" quarterbacks in past years struggled to get past the marks of an average quarterback today.

Table 4.13 The top QB Score quarterbacks in 2019

Rank	*Player*	*QB Score*
1	Patrick Mahomes	2384
2	Dak Prescott	2286
3	Aaron Rodgers	1999
4	Lamar Jackson	1977
5	Russell Wilson	1955
6	Drew Brees	1688
7	Derek Carr	1664
8	Tom Brady	1574
9	Kirk Cousins	1354
10	Kyler Murray	1141
11	Carson Wentz	1140
12	Ryan Tannehill	1095
13	Deshaun Watson	1066
14	Matt Ryan	1051
15	Jared Goff	1046
16	Gardner Minshew II	1041
17	Matthew Stafford	1020
18	Jacoby Brissett	1001
19	Jimmy Garoppolo	887
20	Philip Rivers	748

Do the Best Quarterbacks Win the Super Bowl?

Our discussion of the "best" quarterback and the Super Bowl will consider all 50 of these games since the merger (i.e., from 1970 to 2019).[44] And this discussion will focus on two specific questions.

Does the "best" regular season quarterback win the Super Bowl?

Tom Brady has appeared in nine Super Bowls. In five of these instances, Brady produced more wins in the regular season than the opposing quarterback. And in these five Super Bowls, Brady and the Patriots were victorious three times. Again, Brady has won six Super Bowls. This means in the four instances where he didn't post better regular season numbers he won three times.

[44]The first four Super Bowls (prior to 1970) were contended by teams from two different leagues (the National Football League and the American Football League).

In the twenty-first century this has been the pattern. The team with the best regular season quarterback has been victorious eight times (and lost 12 times). If we look back to 1970, we see that the best and worst quarterbacks have each won 25 times.[45]

> How often does the very best quarterback in the regular season appear and win the Super Bowl?

The previous questions simply compared to the two quarterbacks in the Super Bowl. Fifteen times since 1970 a team has brought to the Super Bowl the quarterback who led all passers in Wins Produced in the regular season. Once again, Patrick Mahomes led all passers in Wins Produced in 2019 and his Chiefs won the Super Bowl. Prior to this victory, though, the last time a top passer won was Peyton Manning in 2006. And prior to Manning, this had only happened six other times since 1970 (Kurt Warner in 1999, Troy Aikman in 1993 and 1995, Steve Young in 1994, Joe Montana in 1989, and Roger Staubach in 1971).

In contrast, nine times a team brought the best passer and lost the Super Bowl. Among this list of quarterbacks is Peyton Manning in 2013, Tom Brady in 2007, Joe Theismann in 1983, and Roger Staubach in 1978. Each of these quarterbacks had won a Super Bowl before that "best" season. And all four still lost the big game.

This suggests a surprising result. Having the "best" quarterback isn't a guarantee of anything. The most common result is the quarterback that produces the most wins in the regular season never even makes it to the Super Bowl. And when they do, these quarterbacks have lost more often than they have won.[46]

[45] A similar result is seen if you look at Wins Produced per 100 plays. The best quarterback in the regular season has won 25 Super Bowls since 1970 (and yes, has lost 25 since 1970).

[46] Berri and Burke (2012) noted a collection of quarterback measures that are "better" than the NFL's quarterback rating. The most widely cited of these is ESPN's QBR metric (based on Brian Burke's work). This measure only goes back to 2006 (so it doesn't work for a study that looks at the history of the Super Bowl). The story, though, is the same. Since 2006, the team with the best QBR quarterback has won six Super Bowls and lost eight. Five times the QBR leader made it to the Super Bowl. That quarterback lost three times. QBR data can be found here: https://www.espn.com/nfl/stats/player/_/season/2019/seasontype/2/table/passing/sort/adjQBR/dir/desc.

What Is the Economic Value of the Face of the Franchise?

So, we have learned two lessons about quarterbacks and the Super Bowl. We just saw that the very best quarterbacks don't always win the Super Bowl. And we learned earlier that winning the Super Bowl appears to increase a quarterback's pay by $2 million.

For most people reading this, $2 million is a great deal of money. But what does this mean for an NFL quarterback? More specifically, how much is $2 million relative to the economic value of an NFL quarterback?

Classic economics argues that workers are paid what they are worth. Therefore, if we want to know the economic value of a quarterback, we simply need to look at salaries. Unfortunately, that simple approach doesn't work in sports.[47]

As Gerald Scully (1974) noted, sports have labor market restrictions that prevent salaries from matching performance. Free agency rights are still not extended to everyone. In addition, payroll caps limit what teams can offer their players. Beyond the labor market restrictions—and similar to what we have already suggested here—Berri et al. (2006) and Berri and Schmidt (2010) noted a number of places where player evaluation in sports does not match the story the data tells. With those two observations in mind, we have to do more than just look at salaries to determine a quarterback's economic value.

Scully (1974) offered the classic approach to making this determination. Scully argued one can measure a baseball player's economic value—or Marginal Revenue Product (MRP)—by estimating two regressions:

- Regress team revenue on team wins (and a collection of other independent variables) to determine the dollar value of an additional win.
- Employ statistical analysis to connect a player's actions on the field to team wins.

[47] It also doesn't work well outside of sports. If you can't measure performance—and in many places that is quite difficult—it would very difficult for a firm to ascertain the "best" worker. And if even if they could, linking output directly to revenue is also immensely challenging. See Berri and Krautmann (2019) for more on the challenges of measuring economic value.

Obviously, this approach can't really work in the NFL. Because teams share so much revenue, it does not appear that an additional win impacts team revenue. In other words—as Berri et al. (2015) found—the issue of fixed revenue (i.e., revenues that don't vary with wins) in the NFL complicates our ability to connect wins to revenue.

As Berri and Krautmann (2019) note, though, even in Major League Baseball the Scully approach doesn't really work very well. Today teams in men's professional sports typically pay about 50% of league revenue to players.[48] When the Scully model is applied to data from the late 1960s, though, it argues that players should be paid more than 100% of the league revenue. When applied to more recent data, though, it argues baseball teams should pay less than one-third of revenue to its players. In sum, the relative value of a win—even when you can statistically find a link between wins and revenue—seems to vary dramatically depending on the time period examined.

Beyond this issue is the fact the Scully model also argues that a player's value is entirely about the number of wins the player produces during the games being played. Bench players who never (or rarely) appear in games have essentially no value according to the Scully approach. Teams, though, pay these players for a reason. You need extra players to conduct practice and as insurance against injury. And that means those players do have value to a team.

Given all these issues, Berri (2014) and Goff (2014) offer an alternative to the Scully model,[49] which we will dub the Berri-Goff approach.[50] Once again, teams in the major men's professional sports tend to pay around 50% of league revenue to their players. Imagine the NFL has \$15 billion in revenue in 2019.[51] The NFL's collective bargaining

[48] As noted in Berri (2015b), Harris and Berri (2016), and Berri (2017b), the WNBA historically has paid less than one-third of its revenue to its players.

[49] This approach was also employed by Berri (2016), Berri (2018), Berri and Krauttmann (2019), and more recently in Garthwaite et al. (2020).

[50] Berri (2014) appeared 10 days in The Atlantic before Goff (2014) appeared at Forbes. It appears the two authors simultaneously came up with this approach to measuring the value of a worker.

[51] Forbes reports that all NFL teams combined to earn \$14.5 billion in revenue in 2018. From 2002 to 2018, Forbes notes that league revenue has increase every year. And the pattern of increase has been remarkably consistent. If we regress current revenue on lagged revenue, we find that 99% of the variation in current total NFL revenue can be explained by last year's revenue and in all but two years the projected revenue from this

agreement says the player receives 48% of league revenue. Therefore, the players should receive $7.2 billion in revenue.

An NFL roster has 53 players. With 32 teams, there are 1696 players employed by the NFL at any given time. The average level of experience for these players is four years[52] and a four-year veteran in the NFL is guaranteed a minimum salary of $720,000.[53] So, we could argue the NFL has guaranteed its players about $1.2 billion in minimum salaries.[54]

The remaining $6 billion in revenue can be distributed according to how many wins the player produced. The NFL has 32 teams playing a 16-game schedule. So, there are 256 regular season wins across the league. Given $6 billion to allocate, each win is worth $23.4 million.

Previously we saw that it was estimated Patrick Mahomes produced 3.0 wins in 2019. As a three-year veteran he was guaranteed $645,000. If we add to that the value of his wins production (i.e., 3.0 multiplied by $23.4 million) we see that Mahomes in 2019 was worth $70.7 million!

Mahomes was the Super Bowl winning quarterback in 2019. And if that is worth $2 million to him, then the Super Bowl victory is worth about 3% of his reported economic value. And that suggests—just as we saw for a team—that winning a Super Bowl isn't worth much to the top quarterbacks.

Unfortunately, there is some reason to think this might not be right. The highest-paid quarterback in 2019 was Matthew Stafford. His cap value was $30.7 million. This methodology says Mahomes was worth more than twice the value of Stafford's pay. In fact—as Table 4.14 indicates—Stafford was worth almost exactly what Stafford was paid. This is surprising, since Stafford only played in eight games in 2019. Despite missing half the season, Stafford—according to this approach—still managed to produce almost as much value than he was paid. That

simple model comes within at least 5% of the what Forbes ultimately reports. When we use this simple model to project 2019 league revenue, we get $15.4 billion in league revenue. For simplicity sake, we will round down for this exercise.

[52] Pells and Fenn (2019).

[53] Zeegers (2019).

[54] That is admittedly a crude calculation. The minimum salary depends on years of experience. Rookies in 2019 were guaranteed $495,000 while players with more than 10 years of experience were guaranteed more than $1 million. The precise amount guaranteed in minimum salaries depends not just on the mean level of experience but the distribution around that mean.

Table 4.14 One view of the most valuable quarterbacks in 2019. Applying the Berri-Goff approach

Rank	*Player*	*Experience*	*Cap number*	*Wins produced*	*Minimum*	*Marginal revenue product*
1	Patrick Mahomes	3	$4,479,808	3.00	$645,000	$70,693,062
2	Dak Prescott	4	$2,120,848	2.75	$720,000	$65,005,378
3	Aaron Rodgers	15	$29,352,000	2.53	$1,030,000	$60,229,449
4	Russell Wilson	8	$26,286,766	2.43	$930,000	$57,668,791
5	Lamar Jackson	2	$2,152,648	2.43	$570,000	$57,219,762
6	Drew Brees	19	$22,700,000	2.13	$1,030,000	$50,806,498
7	Derek Carr	6	$22,500,000	2.00	$806,000	$47,429,586
8	Tom Brady	20	$21,500,000	1.92	$1,030,000	$45,764,848
9	Kirk Cousins	8	$29,000,000	1.61	$930,000	$38,527,342
10	Carson Wentz	4	$8,393,779	1.30	$720,000	$31,141,232
11	Ryan Tannehill	7	$2,225,000	1.29	$806,000	$30,876,596
12	Kyler Murray	1	$6,392,481	1.28	$495,000	$30,370,119
13	Matthew Stafford	11	$30,700,000	1.21	$1,030,000	$29,387,100
14	Gardner Minshew II	1	$542,904	1.20	$495,000	$28,480,051
15	Jacoby Brissett	4	$8,525,000	1.18	$720,000	$28,362,352

suggests the highest-paid quarterback was only being paid for half of his work (had he stayed healthy).

In 2019 there were 72 quarterbacks who we know both their impact on their respective team's cap and who took at least one snap from center. The summation of these player's Marginal Revenue Product is $940 million. The summation of their cap value, though, is $531.6 million. In sum, this group is collectively underpaid by more than $400 million.

It is possible that this is true. But there is also another possibility. The methodology outlined here follows the same approach applied to basketball and baseball. Once again, we utilize the statistics tabulated for the player to calculate their impact on team wins. Then we assign a dollar value to those wins.

The problem in our examination of quarterbacks might be with how wins are calculated. Imagine for a moment we also wanted to calculate the wins produced by a wide receiver. The statistics tracked for a wide receiver include yards from the receptions tabulated for the receiver. But each of those yards is also part of the quarterback's passing yards.

It is important to emphasize this is different in baseball and basketball. If you add up all the hits of a team, you get the team's hits. Add up all the points scored by a team's basketball players, you get the team's points scored. But if you add up all the passing and receiving yards credited to the quarterback(s) and team's receivers, you will get twice the passing yards of the team.

Perhaps we could find a way to split these yards. Maybe we could say the quarterbacks get credit for the yards they throw and receivers only get credit for yards after catch. But even if we could figure out the split between the quarterback and the receiver, how do we determine the contribution of the offensive line?

This is the fundamental problem in analyzing individuals in football. Each play requires the contribution of all the teammates to work. What makes the process even more difficult is that the researcher doesn't even know the play that was called. In other words, from the outside we can't truly tell if a person was doing their job correctly (or incorrectly) because we can't know for sure what their job was. We see an interception on the field. But we can't know if the it happened because the quarterback made a mistake or the receiver ran the wrong route.[55]

All of this gets us back to something we have already noted. The statistics tracked for the quarterbacks are remarkably inconsistent. Once again, this is because their performance depends on the players around the quarterback. This inconsistency doesn't just make it difficult for teams to know

[55] There is another possibility. The quarterback knows the other team's defense. But one suspects sometimes an interception happens because a defensive player doesn't know the defense and therefore ends up in the "wrong" place; which just happens to be a place the quarterback was throwing to because they knew that defensive player wouldn't be there!

how a quarterback will perform in the future, it also makes it very difficult for one to objectively determine a quarterback's economic value.

Economists have historically argued that workers are generally paid their Marginal Revenue Product. To see if this is true, though, one has to be able to measure MRP. One would think in football—where performance is measured and revenue of teams reported—this would certainly be possible. But in the end, we see that in an environment where you can't clearly separate the contribution of workers from each other, measuring MRP can't be done.

In the end, maybe this simple investigation of the Super Bowl is telling us a bigger story. In many workplaces people work as teams to produce output. Our study of football indicates that in a world where people interact to create something, we can guess what MRP might be for each worker. But it is unlikely we can know with certainty.

So, what is the value of Patrick Mahomes, Tom Brady, and the other quarterbacks we have examined? There is reason to think the team's evaluations aren't quite right. But in the end, it isn't possible for us to say with certainty what is right.[56]

Concluding Thoughts

In North America, the Super Bowl is the largest televised sporting event.[57] Winning this game clearly means quite a bit to the athletes. We were interested, though, in the financial value of victory.

Because the NFL shares more than 60% of its revenue, the value of winning the Super Bowl for a team is relatively small. The winning team appears to see its revenue increase by a mere $13 million. Of course, at least that is something. We also learned that winning NFL games doesn't seem to have any impact on team revenue.

As for players, our focus was on the "face of the franchise." We saw evidence that winning a Super Bowl could increase the pay of the winning

[56]That might mean that the NFL evaluations are ultimately correct. Of course, we can't independently verify whether or not that is true. Given what we have seen in other sports—where we can measure individual performance more precisely—there isn't much reason to think decision-making in the NFL is much different.

[57]Berri (2018) notes that the Super Bowl doesn't draw anywhere near the television audience of top soccer matches around the world. Soccer—or real football—has a much bigger worldwide audience than American football.

quarterback by about $2 million. That winning quarterback, though, was usually not the best quarterback in the regular season. In fact, the very best quarterback in the regular season often didn't win the Super Bowl.

It appears the value of those best quarterbacks is far beyond the pay of these players. In fact, it appears that the $2 million estimated payout from winning the Super Bowl is quite insignificant relative to the economic value of these players.

Unfortunately—and this has to be remembered when we do empirical studies of football—estimating the value of an individual in a team sport where outcomes depend so much on teammate interaction is quite difficult. And that means, it is likely our estimates of a quarterback's economic value are incorrect. Unfortunately, it is also likely that the final question we asked in this chapter isn't one we can precisely answer.

That doesn't mean we know nothing. Table 4.14 does give us a ranking of quarterbacks and that ranking suggests Patrick Mahomes and Dak Prescott offered more to their respective teams in 2019 than Tom Brady and Kirk Cousins. Were they worth $30 million more? Well, we probably can't say that. But we might be able to say they were worth more!

References

Berri, D.. (2007). Back to Back Evaluation on the Gridiron. In J. H. Albert & R. H. Koning (Eds.), *Statistical Thinking in Sport* (pp. 235–256). Boca Raton: Chapman & Hall/CRC.

Berri, D. (2008). A Simple Measure of Worker Productivity in the National Basketball Association. In B. Humphreys & D. Howard (Eds.), *The Business of Sport* (3 vols., pp. 1–40). Westport, CT: Praeger.

Berri, D. (2014, March 21). If We Paid NCAA Basketball Players What They're Really Worth, This Is What They'd Earn: And Here's a Cockamamie Plan to Get It for Them. *The Atlantic*. http://www.theatlantic.com/business/archive/2014/03/if-we-paid-ncaa-basketball-players-what-theyre-really-worth-this-is-what-theyd-earn/284559/.

Berri, D. (2015a, March 26). American's Socialist Sports League: The NFL. *The Atlantic*. http://www.theatlantic.com/business/archive/2015/03/americas-socialist-sports-league-thenfl/388330/.

Berri, D. (2015b, August 12). Basketball's Gender Wage Gap Is Even Worse Than You Think. *Vice Sports*. https://sports.vice.com/en_us/article/basketballs-gender-wage-gap-is-even-worse-than-you-think.

Berri, D. (2016). Paying NCAA Athletes. *Marquette Sports Law Review, 26*(2).

Berri, D. (2017a, February 7). Parallel Universes and Our Perceptions of Tom Brady. *Huffington Post*. http://www.huffingtonpost.com/entry/parallel-universes-and-our-perceptions-of-tom-brady_us_5899efc6e4b0c1284f2845d9.

Berri, D. (2017b, September 20). Basketball's Growing Gender Gap: The Evidence the WNBA Is Underpaying Players. *Forbes*. https://www.forbes.com/sites/davidberri/2017/09/20/there-is-a-growing-gender-wage-gap-in-professional-basketball/#435aea1536e0.

Berri, D. (2018). *Sports Economics*. New York, NY: Worth Publishers/Macmillan Education.

Berri, D. (2019). 'The Answer' and the Economics of Basketball: Perceptions vs Production. In P. Downward, B. Frick, B. R. Humphreys, T. Pawlowski, J. E. Ruseski, & B. P. Soebbing (Eds.), *The Sage Handbook of the Economics of Sports* (pp. 279–288). London: Sage.

Berri, D. J., & Burke, B. (2012). Measuring Performance in the NFL. In *The Economics of the National Football League* (pp. 137–158). New York, NY: Springer.

Berri, D. J., & Krautmann, A. C. (2019). How Much Did Baseball's Antitrust Exemption Cost Bob Gibson?. *The Antitrust Bulletin, 64*(4), 566–583.

Berri, D., Leeds, M., & von Allmen, P. (2015, February). Salary Determination in the Presence of Fixed Revenues. *International Journal of Sport Finance, 10*, 5–25.

Berri, D., & Schmidt, M. (2010). *Stumbling on Wins: Two Economists Explore the Pitfalls on the Road to Victory in Professional Sports*. Princeton, NJ: Financial Times Press.

Berri, D., Schmidt, M., & Brook, S. L. (2006). *The Wages of Wins: Taking Measure of the Many Myths in Modern Sport*. Stanford University Press. Released in paperback in September, 2007.

Berri, D., & Simmons, R. (2009, February). Race and the Evaluation of Signal Callers in the National Football League. *Journal of Sports Economics, 10*(1), 23–43.

Berri, D., & Simmons, R. (2011, February). Catching a Draft: On the Process of Selecting Quarterbacks in the National Football League Amateur Draft. *Journal of Productivity Analysis, 35*(1), 37–49. https://doi.org/10.1007/s11123-009-0154-6.

Berri, D., Simmons, R., Van Gilder, J., & O'Neill, L. (2011). What Does It Mean to Find the Face of the Franchise? Physical Attractiveness and the Evaluation of Athletic Performance. *Economics Letters., 111*, 200–202.

Blass, A. (1992). Does the Baseball Labor Market Contradict the Human Capital Model? *Review of Economics and Statistics, 74*, 261–268.

Bloom, H. (2014, September 5). NFL Revenue-Sharing Model Good for Business. *Sporting News*. https://www.sportingnews.com/us/nfl/news/nfl-revenue-sharing-television-contracts-2014-season-business-model-nba-nhl-mlb-comparison-salary-cap/gu0xok7mphu01x3vu875oeaq6.

Coster, H. (2020, February 3). Super Bowl TV Audience Rises Slightly to 99.9 Million Viewers. *Reuters News*. https://www.reuters.com/article/us-football-nfl-superbowl-ratings/super-bowl-tv-audience-rises-slightly-to-99-9-million-viewers-idUSKBN1ZX2LI.

Fitzgerald, J. (2013, February 13). *A Guide to the NFL Salary Cap*. https://overthecap.com/a-guide-to-the-nfl-salary-cap/.

Fitzgerald, J. (2018, September 5). 2018 Spending in the NFL by Team. *Over the Cap*. https://overthecap.com/2018-spending-on-nfl-rosters/.

Forrest, D., & Simmons, R. (2006). New Issues in Attendance Demand. The Case of the English Football League. *Journal of Sports Economics, 7*(3), 247–266.

Garthwaite, C., Keener, J., Notowidigdo, M. J., & Ozminkowski, N. (2020, August). *Who Profits from Amateurism? Rent-Sharing in Modern College Sports* (Working paper).

Gerrard, B. (2007). Is the Moneyball Approach Transferable to Complex Invasion Team Sports? *International Journal of Sports Finance, 2,* 214–228.

Goff, B. (2014, March 31). The Market Value of NCAA Athletes in the Millions. *Forbes*. https://www.forbes.com/sites/briangoff/2014/03/31/the-market-value-of-ncaa-athletes-in-the-millions/#2cf626e57948.

Harris, J., & Berri, D. (2016, August). If You Can't Pay Them, Play Them: Fan Preference and Own-Race Bias in the WNBA. *International Journal of Sport Finance, 11,* 163–180.

Klein, C. (2019, January 30). The Bizarre History of the NFL's First Title Game. *History. A&E Television Networks*. https://www.history.com/news/the-bizarre-history-of-the-nfls-first-title-game.

McCraken, V. (2001). *Pitching and Defense: How Much Control Do Hurlers Have?* http://www.baseballprospectus.com/article.php?articleid=878.

Ourand, J. (2020, March 23). NFL Presses Toward Massive New Media Deals, with Formal Negotiations Near. *Street&Smiths Sports Business Journal*. https://www.sportsbusinessdaily.com/Journal/Issues/2020/03/23/Sports-and-Society/NFL-mediaCV.aspx.

Pells, E., & Fenn, L. (2019, January 27). AP Analysis: The NFL Keeps Going Younger and Cheaper. *The Associated Press*. https://apnews.com/116b7142400240b8852330eedbd82d6d.

Scully, G. (1974). Pay and Performance in Major League Baseball. *American Economic Review, 64,* 915–930.

Zeegers, M. (2019, September 30). What Is the NFL's League Minimum Salary for 2019? *Sportscasting*. https://www.sportscasting.com/what-is-the-nfls-league-minimum-salary-for-2019/.

CHAPTER 5

The Performers

Abstract The NFL produces an expensive halftime show in order to maintain its large television audience. The artists who preform at halftime are barely compensated by the NFL. An exploration of the benefits to the performer in the areas of music consumption and future concert revenues were tested using the sign test. Music consumption was found to significantly increase following the halftime show. Concert data did not show the same level of significance, but the amount of data available was small. The lack of pay for cheerleaders is also considered here. Mercantilist opportunities for the NFL in charging the halftime act to perform were explored. If the image of the league to fans is important to the NFL, then using a nested game approach the league would choose not to charge artists.

Keywords Exploitation · Bargaining power · Song consumption · Nested games · Gross concert revenue · Mercantilism

Annually, the NFL championship game, the Super Bowl, is one of the most watched televised events in the United States (Super Bowl Ratings History 2020). In studies of this cultural phenomenon, the sports economics literature tends to focus on the game and who hosts it. But this

Y. J. Kelly et al., *The Economics of the Super Bowl*, Palgrave Pivots in Sports Economics, https://doi.org/10.1007/978-3-030-46370-0_5

entertainment spectacle has two additional elements: the halftime show and NFL cheerleaders.

The halftime show is a small industry by itself. It has direct ties to the television ratings of the game, as well as to the expenses for the NFL in producing the game. In addition, the artists who are chosen to perform at the halftime show receive financial benefits from their appearance. This chapter will examine the halftime show and the benefits that come to those performers. The chapter will also explore the mercantilist opportunities that are present for the NFL and the reasons why the league should or should not exploit those opportunities at the Super Bowl.

As for cheerleaders, it is important to remember that 47% of NFL fans are women (Johnson 2020). Historically, though, women who wanted to work in the NFL didn't have many opportunities for jobs outside the job of cheerleader. And historically, as we will show, that has led to a fair amount of both economic and non-economic exploitation.

The purpose of this chapter is to explore the economics of these performers who don't actively participate in the playing of the football game. More importantly, we wish to highlight how bargaining power can dramatically alter the outcomes we observe. We will begin with a detailed discussion of the halftime show, where we will show the NFL doesn't end up with a very good deal because it lacks bargaining power. The chapter will then contrast this story with a discussion of the market for NFL cheerleaders where the NFL has—and is willing to exploit—the immense bargaining power it possesses.

Halftime Show History

In the early years of the Super Bowl, from 1967 to 1992, the halftime show was not a highly featured element of the broadcast of the game. The halftime coverage was mostly devoted to a studio analysis of the first half of the game and had some brief cut-ins of the halftime show on the field. During those years, college marching bands performed at halftime in 15 of the 25 years (Sports Illustrated 2017). Other acts that were selected to perform would provide a broad acceptance, but perhaps not provide a broad excitement. This genre of acts included singing groups such as Up With People, which performed at the Super Bowl four times (Sports Illustrated 2017).

The importance and the scale of the halftime show changed significantly following the events of the 1992 game. That year, the game was televised on CBS but a rival television network, FOX, heavily advertised that it was having an extravagant halftime show which would feature the cast of its popular comedy show In Living Color. This alternative halftime show proved to be very attractive to the viewers of the Super Bowl who turned away from CBS and tuned in FOX during halftime. CBS saw halftime ratings drop from a 40.2 rating the previous year to 32.8 for that 1992 game (Nielsen 2018).

Following this incident, both the NFL and the broadcasters of the game wanted to ensure that in future games they would maintain their large audience through halftime. Their goal was to deliver to the advertisers the viewership numbers that the advertisers anticipated, expected, and paid for. To maintain the audience during the following year, 1993, the NFL responded with a halftime show featuring the very popular singer Michael Jackson. That show saw ratings rebound from 32.8 to 45.6 (Nielsen 2018). This show set a halftime ratings record that would stand until a 2012 performance by Madonna, which broke the record with a rating of 46.9 (Nielsen 2018).

Since that 1992 Michael Jackson show, popular music has been emphasized in the halftime show by featuring hit makers. Headliners of the show have included artists such as Bruno Mars (2014), Lady Gaga (2017), and Katy Perry (2015) as well as classic, legacy rock acts such as Paul McCartney (2005), The Who (2010), and Bruce Springsteen (2009) (Newman 2019). The selection of the halftime act is made by the NFL. The sponsor of the halftime show (currently Pepsi) and the network which is broadcasting the game are both consulted by the NFL about the selection of the performers (Newman 2019).

Costs of the Halftime Show

The NFL pays the production costs of the halftime show (Quenzel 2019). While popular media have estimated that these costs can be as high as $10 million per show (Cassels 2018), the actual costs are not made public by the NFL. While not revealing a figure, a Senior Vice President for Programming and Production for the NFL indicated that the $10 million estimate was low (Quenzel 2019). The attorney of a recent Super Bowl performer, who requested anonymity, revealed that the cost for the production of his or her client's show was more in the neighborhood of $25 million.

If that figure is correct, the show costs more than $2 million dollars per minute to produce. The high costs are in part due to the show being tough to design. Start by looking at the stage used. The stage, which is built by entirely union labor, must have lights, lifts, multi-levels, pyrotechnics, must have enough structural integrity to support all the stage activity. In addition, it must have the fidelity to look good for television, and, must be able to be dismantled and removed from the field within 12 minutess.

Aside from the stage itself, the production expenses include sound, lighting, stadium pyrotechnics, costumes, security, musicians, and dancers. In addition, the featured artist of the halftime show can negotiate with the NFL concerning the expenses involved in bringing their "glam squad." A glam squad consists of the artist's hair, makeup, and wardrobe personnel. One artist brought with them an 11-member glam squad, whose flights, hotels, and meals were all paid for by the NFL.

One of the costs that is negligible for the NFL is the actual pay to the star performer. Performers are paid according the union scale of the Screen Actors Guild-American Federation of Television and Radio Artists (SAG-AFTRA) for a live television performance. In the latest update to the 2014–2020 SAG-AFTRA contract, that scale rate is $584 (SAG-AFTRA 2018). This scale amount is far, far less than what an artist who has the popularity level to be considered as a Super Bowl performer would generate in revenue from a typical concert. As an example, Bruno Mars, who was the headline halftime performer in 2014, averaged $2.6 million in gross revenues per concert in 2018 (Allen 2018). Practically speaking, by only paying the halftime artist the SAG-AFTRA union scale amount, the NFL does not really pay the star performers. However, in most years artists consider it to be an honor to be selected as the halftime act, despite this lack of direct pay (Cassels 2018).

Given the large opportunity cost involved, considering that the artist could have given a more profitable concert elsewhere on the day of the game, performing at the Super Bowl could be considered a volunteer effort by the artist. This raises the question as to why the performer would basically agree to play for free.

In examining why a performer would agree to not be compensated at his or her typical rate, it is theorized that the performers accept the invitation to perform at the Super Bowl in exchange for the promotional value of being televised to such a very large worldwide audience. The result of their performing is an increase in the exposure for the artist. This added exposure should lead to an increase in the demand for their music, resulting in a boost in music sales and streaming, the sale of future concert tickets, and also in future product endorsement deals. This potential boost in income would make it worthwhile for the artists to volunteer to perform at the halftime show.

Benefits of Performing and Song Consumption

The halftime show has a running time between 12 and 13 ½ minutes. If the show is viewed from the perspective of being a promotional event for the performing artist, then the show can be considered as a lengthy advertisement for that artist. An advantage for the performer is that they do not have to pay the advertising rates for this air time during the Super Bowl. Because the audience is large, advertising rates for commercials during the broadcast of the Super Bowl are steep.

The price of thirty-second ads during the broadcast are set by the broadcasting network and are formulated considering the size and the demographics of the audience being provided to the advertisers (Raithela et al. 2016). The equivalent advertising value of the halftime show can be found by multiplying the length of the halftime show by the thirty-second ad rate for that year. Table 5.1, shows the equivalent advertising value for the Super Bowl performers from 2014 to 2017. The advertising rates are inflation adjusted to 2017 dollars (Johnson 2017).

What remains to be explored is the extent to which this type of advertising generates revenues for the performers. To evaluate this, a methodology similar to that which had been used to measure the success of products advertised during the Super Bowl is utilized. Hartman and Klapper (2017) examined sales for beer and soda products that were advertised during the game. They measured sales for the products for each of the seven days prior to the game, sales for the day of the game, and sales

Table 5.1 Equivalent advertising value for the Super Bowl performers from 2014 to 2017

Year	*Show length*	*Cost per :30 ad*	*Equivalent advertising value*
2014	13:12	$4,340,000	$114,576,000
2015	12:35	$4,551,000	$114,533,500
2016	13:12	$4,898,000	$129,307,200
2017	13:34	$5,000,000	$135,666,667

for the seven days following the game. Their findings showed statistically significant increases in sales for the brands of beer and soda advertised during the game (Hartman and Klapper 2017). Using that methodology, the impact that performing at halftime has on the consumption of the artists' music can be estimated, provided that the equivalent data can be located.

It turns out that finding data on music consumption is very difficult and also very expensive. The Billboard charts are not helpful for a project such as this. People can look at the Hot 100 charts in Billboard magazine and see what the number one song of the week is. What is not revealed in that chart is the amount of that song which was consumed. A song could be number one this week but have a fraction of the consumption that the song which was number one the previous week had.

In addition, it is not revealed in that chart number what the mix was of the consumption of the song. We do not know how many times the song was downloaded as a purchase, streamed on a service such as Spotify, or viewed in a video such as on YouTube. This mix is important because each method pays different rates the artist. To dig deeper into music consumption numbers requires access to industry databases and proprietary information. Doing so was beyond the resources of these researchers.

The difficulty in obtaining data limited the number of observations available for this study. Nielsen Music has data available that may have been useful in a study such as this, however the cost of utilizing their database far exceeded the research budget of this study. Nielsen has a rival in the data collection industry, BuzzAngle. BuzzAngle is a music analytics firm founded in 2013. Insiders in the music industry, who preferred not to be named, said they prefer BuzzAngle because their data is more timely and also, in their opinion, more accurate. In 2019, BuzzAngle partnered with Rolling Stone magazine to provide the data needed to construct that magazine's music charts (Christman 2019).

Utilizing data from the BuzzAngle (2017) annual music report, the total track equivalent consumption of music for each of the halftime performing artists from 2014 to 2017 was examined. In music industry parlance, a track means a song. Total track equivalent consumption is the total number of times the song was purchased, streamed, or viewed. BuzzAngle utilizes a formula to assign weights for each of these types of consumption. The total number of streams is equal to the number of audio streams divided by 150 plus the number of video streams divided by 150, as shown in this formula:

$$\text{Streams} = \text{Audio streams}/150 + \text{Video streams}/150$$

Total track equivalent consumption is the number of paid song downloads plus the adjusted number of streams:

$$\text{Track Equivalent Consumption} = \text{Downloads} + \text{Streams}$$

Part of the reason for the weighting adjustment with the number of streams is that 1 million streams is not financially equivalent to sales from 1 million downloads. Thus, to accurately award gold records for 500,000 units consumed, the audio and video streaming totals need adjustment. The weighting adjustment brings the two sources, purchases and streams, closer for comparison purposes. A similar formula is used by Billboard in determining its Hot 100 songs of the week.

The data provided by BuzzAngle are the total track equivalent consumption figures for the artists. This track consumption was measured for each day of the week prior to the Super Bowl game, the day of the game, and also for each day of the week following the game. Since music consumption on the day of the game will be considered to be part of the beneficial boost for the artists for performing at the game, the data is categorized here into two groups. One group is the daily average for the seven days pre-Super Bowl and the other group is the daily average for the game day plus the seven days following the game.

Table 5.2 reveals the bump in song consumption for the artists who performed at the Super Bowl from 2014 to 2017. These data are for

Table 5.2 Daily weighted song consumption

Year	*Artist*	*Week prior to Super Bowl daily average*	*Game Day + 7 day daily average*
2014	Bruno Mars	1,215,321	2,769,844
	Red Hot Chili Peppers	315,536	350,906
2015	Katy Perry	1,150,179	2,386,875
	Missy Elliott	28,500	748,125
	Lenny Kravitz	580,179	1,425,000
2016	Coldplay	1,119,643	2,139,281
	Beyoncé	690,107	722,297
2017	Lady Gaga	488,571	3,072,656

music consumption in the United States alone. The first name listed for each year is the headlining performer for that year. The names appearing below that of the headliner were featured guests in the halftime show for that year.

While these figures show an increase in song consumption for each artist, there is still a need to estimate the dollar value of this consumption. Determining the dollar value of this daily weighted song consumption presents some difficulties because the track equivalent consumption figures that were provided by BuzzAngle conflate song streams, views, and sales. Each of these consumption methods pays the artists a different royalty amount. According to BuzzAngle, approximately 85% of songs were streamed or viewed as opposed to being purchased (BuzzAngle 2017). To further complicate things, the rates paid to artists for streaming varies by streaming company. Thus, coming up with a determinate value is difficult; however, reasonable estimates can be made.

Spotify, the largest streaming service, accounts for 51.51% of streams and pays $0.00397 per stream (Katz 2018). Apple, which makes up 22.29% of the streaming market, pays $0.00783 per stream (Katz 2018). Pandora, which provides 7.86% of streams, pays $0.00134 per stream (Katz 2018). These three streaming services make up 81.7% of the total streaming market (Sanchez 2018). Royalties for videos of songs played on YouTube are substantially smaller. YouTube pays $0.00074 per stream (Sanchez 2018). To additionally complicate matters, some streaming services pay higher royalties for songs streamed or viewed by customers who have paid subscription accounts verses those royalties paid when streamed or viewed by customers who utilize free accounts. The number of streams from paid accounts vs. the number of streams from free accounts is not publicly available. Therefore, the royalty payments used in this study are generalized, conservative estimates using the lower tier of the payment values.

Instances where songs are purchased are easier to estimate revenues. A song that is downloaded and purchased via iTunes, pays the artist 70% of the revenue generated. Therefore, a song which sells for $1.29 on iTunes will result in payment to the artist of $0.903 cents (Songcast 2019).

Acknowledging that each artist may have their songs consumed in differing ratios, all artists here are treated as representative agents (Osborne and Rubinstein 1994). A weighted average is constructed by taking the payment from each source and multiplying it by the percentage of song consumption from that source. Multiplying audio streaming payments from Spotify, Apple, and Pandora, by the percentage of song consumption that comes from each source, the payment for audio streaming would equal $0.0047 per stream. Using that same technique for video streaming, YouTube would average a weighted payment of $0.00027 per view. Purchased songs would provide a weighted average of $0.1106 per song. Added together, the total estimated track equivalent generates a value of approximately $0.1156 to the performer. Table 5.3 is a table of the average daily value of weighted song consumption for the seven days prior to the Super Bowl and game day plus seven days after. These values are adjusted to 2017 dollars.

Each of the artists show an increase in the average daily revenue from their music. Some, such as Lady Gaga, show tremendous increases. Lady Gaga, for instance, went from $56,464 per day in song consumption prior to the game, to $355,107 per day following the game.

Artists, of course, do not keep the entirety of these funds they earn. Aside from taxes, they must make payments from revenues to their agents, managers, publicists, publishing companies, attorneys, and record labels. As an example of how this money is distributed, an attorney for a recent Super Bowl performer stated that for each $1 of revenue generated by the artist for streams on Spotify, 30 cents is kept by Spotify, 10 cents goes to the publisher of the song (which it then shares with the songwriter), leaving 60 cents to go to the artist. The artist then typically splits that 60 cents on a 50/50 basis with their record label. Some highly successful artists are able to negotiate a 60/40 split with their label. Other members of the artist's team are the paid from the remaining 30 cents. Income

Table 5.3 Average daily value of weighted song consumption

Year	*Artist*	*Average daily value Pre-Super Bowl*	*Average daily value Game day + 7*
2014	Bruno Mars	$145,812	$322,321
	Red Hot Chili Peppers	$37,857	$42,101
2015	Katy Perry	$138,130	$286,630
	Missy Elliott	$3,421	$89,839
	Lenny Kravitz	$69,671	$171,122
2016	Coldplay	$132,632	$253,417
	Beyonce	$81,545	$85,563
2017	Lady Gaga	$56,464	$355,107

from other sources also face similar distributions. So, while it is shown that artists generate large sums of money following their performance, it does not mean that these funds all end up in the artist's pocket.

Because the data was not selected randomly from a larger pool of data, a non-parametric method of testing for statistical significance was used. The data for each artist was summed into two groups, one group for the total amount of songs consumed the seven days prior to the Super Bowl and the other group for the songs consumed the day of the game plus seven days. A sign test was performed on the data. This test was appropriate to use given the small number of observations. The sign test has two conditions: the two groups are paired and the pairs are independent of other pairs (Anderson et al. 1999). Since this is a before and after situation, and since each artist is independent of each other artist from year to year, the conditions for the test were met.

Using the sign test, the difference in the median for each pair of data for each artist was examined. If performing at the Super Bowl was not significant in boosting song consumption, then half of the median differences would be expected to be positive and half of the median differences would be expected to be negative. The null hypothesis is that the median sign difference in the song consumption per artist in the two groups from the 7 days before the Super Bowl, and game day plus 7 days after the game, is zero. In other words, the number of plus signs would be expected to be the same as the number of negative signs. This null hypothesis says that the artist's participation in the Super Bowl halftime show had no effect on his or her career.

The alternate hypothesis is that that median sign difference in the song consumption per artist from the 7 days before the Super Bowl and the game day plus 7 days after the Super Bowl is different than zero. The alternate hypothesis implies that the artist's participation in the Super Bowl halftime show had an effect, either positive or negative, on his or her career. A net positive would indicate performing at the Super Bowl had a positive effect on his or her career and a net negative would indicate performing at the Super Bowl had a negative effect on his or her career. The null and alternative hypotheses are presented as:

H_0 = the median difference is zero (half the differences are positive and half are negative)
H_1 = the median difference is not zero (there are more than 50% positive or negative)

Table 5.4 Song Consumption sign test results

Variable	n	Sample median	Below	Equal	Above	*p*-value
Differences	8	865890	0	0	8	0.0039

Results

There were eight paired observations used to test the hypothesis. An alpha level of .01 was chosen as the level of significance. Subtracting the median for the group of the 7 days before the game from the median of the group for the game day plus 7 for each artist resulted in 8 positive observations. The sign test results are shown in Table 5.4.

The *p*-value of 0.0039 indicates that there is only a 0.39% chance of having a sample of 8 halftime performers indicating that their career was positively enhanced by participating in the halftime show if, in actuality, the halftime show had no effect on their career. Since the *p*-value of .0039 is less than the alpha level of significance (0.01), the null hypothesis is rejected. The findings support the alternate hypothesis; it does not appear that this situation happened by chance alone. The test suggests that performing at halftime of the Super Bowl was beneficial to the artists.

Benefits of Performing at Halftime and Future Concerts

Music consumption is only one part of the revenue stream for a performing artist. As album sales of Compact Discs (CD) dwindled, the main source of income for music artists has become live performances (Krueger 2019). This development is a rather recent and important change in the music industry. It used to be that an artist would undertake a concert tour in support of a new album they had released. The concert tour was designed to develop new fans and to entice those who attended to buy the new album. During the time of this concert model, the average price of a concert ticket in 1981 was $12 (Krueger 2019).

This market environment changed substantially in 1999 with the founding of Napster. People used the Napster software service for peer-to-peer music file sharing, acquiring music at no charge. The result was that CD sales plummeted. Consumers chose not to pay for a physical product when they could download the same music for free, even though this violated copyright laws. Court rulings shut down Napster in 2001. By this time CD sales had not only diminished but consumer preferences had changed. Rather than buying an entire album, consumers changed to instead buying only the songs they wanted (Krueger 2019). In 2003, this consumer demand was met, but this time in a legal way. That year, Apple created the iTunes store where individual songs could be purchased. In 2008, the Spotify streaming service began. Using the Spotify service, consumers could stream songs legally by paying a monthly fee to do so (Ku 2002). In addition to the subscription service, Spotify also offered a free service that required the listener to occasionally hear commercials between songs. The rise of streaming saw a decrease in income from music sales for artists which led to the evolution of concerts and ticket prices.

Concerts became more elaborate. Improvements in sound, lighting, staging, and pyrotechnics made the stage shows a spectacle of entertainment. Along with the increase in production value came an increase in ticket prices. By 2017, the average face value price of a concert ticket had grown to $69 (Krueger 2019). The goal of new music released by artists was to draw people to their concerts. The tour was no longer designed to support the album, the album was now designed to support the tour. This was a reversal of the previous live music market.

In order to look at the impact that being the Super Bowl halftime performer had on concert sales, a similar approach to that used for song consumption is employed. This approach, though, is slightly modified. Concert data for the same artists included in the previous song consumption section are used here. The data includes the number of shows, the number of tickets sold, and the gross amount from ticket sales per artist. The data are generally available (and for a researcher, also affordable) from the Pollstar box office data.

The validity of Pollstar data was examined, confirmed, and presented by Krueger in his book *Rockonomics* (2019). He examined the number of shows reported and compared it to concert listings found on setlist.com as well as employing some confidential data which had been made available to him. His conclusion was that the Pollstar data was accurate, and that its reporting of price and revenue data was reliable (Krueger 2019). For this study, however, the data once again became an obstacle.

The initial intent was to take the same artists who had performed in the 2014–2017 Super Bowls and to measure the average gross ticket sales for each artist one year prior to their performance at the Super Bowl and one year following the game. As simple as that sounds, collecting that data presented problems. First, just to be considered to be the Super Bowl halftime performer the artist must be, at some level, considered a star performer. Star performers are often offered opportunities to play at premier events. These artists are hired to perform at large festivals such as Coachella, Summerfest, South by Southwest (SXSW), Bonaroo, and others. It is difficult for a researcher to establish what percentage of ticket sales for a three-day event should be attributed to an artist who plays only one set on one night. The revenue from these festivals can be quite large. As an example, in 2013, following their appearance at the Super Bowl, the Red Hot Chili Peppers played at Coachella. The festival had gross revenues of $67,208,033 that year. The portion of that revenue which was generated solely because of the appearance of the Red Hot Chili Peppers is impossible to discern. As such, data from that festival was dropped from the data set. This dropping of festival data was also done for each of the other artists who similarly played at large festivals. The problem is that many of these artists played at many of these festivals, both here and internationally, resulting in a many data points being dropped from the data set.

The second problem with the concert revenue data is missing data. Because these artists are internationally known, their concert tours include overseas shows. While Pollstar was able to capture the dates of these international shows, information about ticket prices, attendance, and revenue information was not always included in their data. As a result, these concerts were not included in the data set for this study. This became a big problem by greatly reducing the remaining data available for some artists. For example, the year after playing at the Super Bowl, Bruno Mars had 85 concerts that year, however 20 of those had no revenue data. In 2015, Lenny Kravitz had 45 concerts, but data was only available for 8 of them. Of interest, outside of the United States, European concerts had the most available data, South American concerts were inconsistent, and Asian concerts had the least amount of available data.

Of the eight artists included in this study, one did not have concert data at all. Missy Elliot did not perform at any concerts the year prior to, or for the year she performed at the Super Bowl. Since she no longer tours, her Super Bowl performance took on a special significance. However, as far as the data set for this part of the study, she was removed from it.

One last difficulty with the concert data was that three of the artists, Lady Gaga, Coldplay, and Beyoncé did not tour the year prior to playing at the Super Bowl. Artists take time off from touring so that they can record new albums, work on other projects such as movies, or simply take a break after working hard to achieve their level of success. To adjust for this, the pre-Super Bowl data for those three artists included data from concerts held two years prior to their appearance at the Super Bowl. Even then, Coldplay only played eight concerts, four of which were festivals and which were dropped from the data set.

The available data for concerts following the Super Bowl performances saw equal troubles. The Red Hot Chili Peppers played only 6 concerts the year following their Super Bowl appearance and only one of those had data that could be included in the data set. As stated previously, Lenny Kravitz had 45 concerts the following year, but only 8 of those had data that could be included in the data set.

What seemed like an easy pre and post-Super Bowl sign test turned out to be not very easy because of the very limited data. Table 5.5 displays the number of concerts per artist for the year pre and post-Super Bowl performance, the average gross revenue per show, and also the number

Table 5.5 Concerts per artist one year before and year after Super Bowl appearance

Year	*Artist*	*Shows pre-Super Bowl*	*Average gross revenue*	*Shows with no data or festivals*	*Shows post-Super Bowl*	*Average gross revenue*	*Shows with no data or festivals*
2014	Bruno Mars	80	$880,353	7	65	$1,126,567	20
	Red Hot Chili Peppers	12	$1,730,476	9	1	$1,124,680	5
2015	Katy Perry	107	$1,422,746	1	42	$1,186,722	2
	Missy Elliot	0	$0	0	0	$0	0
	Lenny Kravitz	11	$642,142	21	8	$188,775	37
2016	Coldplay	4[a]	$204,073	4	120	$4,413,096	2
	Beyoncé	46[a]	$3,265,170	4	50	$5,151,563	1
2017	Lady Gaga	78[a]	$1,056,196	12	49	$1,926,643	10

[a]Shows held two years prior to Super Bowl appearance
Source Pollstar

of concerts which were either dropped from the data set or had missing data.

In order to perform the sign test, it needed to be determined which artists provided enough data to be included in the test. Missy Elliot with no data was excluded from the test. The Red Hot Chili Peppers and Lenny Kravitz were also excluded. It was decided that since those artists had more concerts where there was no data, than there were concerts where there was viable data, it was best to exclude them from the test. In the case of the Red Hot Chili Peppers, they only had one post-Super Bowl concert that could be included. A single data point is not appropriate for purposes of the sign test.

Methodology and Significance

Using the sign test, the difference in the median for each pair of data for each artist was examined for their pre-Super Bowl appearance average gross revenue per concert and their post-Super Bowl appearance average gross revenue per concert. If performing at the Super Bowl was not significant in boosting average per concert revenues, then half of the median differences would be expected to be positive and half of the median differences would be expected to be negative. The null hypothesis therefore is that the median sign difference in the average per concert gross revenue is zero. In other words, the number of plus signs would be expected to be the same as the number of negative signs. This null hypothesis implies that the artist's participation in the Super Bowl halftime show had no effect on his or her concert career.

The alternate hypothesis is that the median sign difference in the average per concert gross revenue is different than zero. This alternate hypothesis implies that the artist's participation in the Super Bowl halftime show had an effect, either positive or negative, on his or her concert career. A net positive would indicate performing at the Super Bowl had a positive effect on his or her concert career and a net negative would indicate performing at the Super Bowl had a negative effect on his or her concert career. The null and alternative hypotheses are presented as:

> H_0 = the median difference is zero (half the differences are positive and half are negative)
> H_1 = the median difference is not zero (there are more than 50% positive or negative)

There were only five paired observations used to test the hypothesis. An alpha level of .01 was chosen as the level of significance. Subtracting the median for the average per concert gross revenue for the year before their appearance at the halftime show of the Super Bowl from the median of the average per concert gross revenue for the year following the Super Bowl for each artist resulted in 4 positive observations and 1 negative observation. The sign test results are shown in Table 5.6.

The *p*-value of 0.1875 indicates that there is an 18.7% chance of having a sample of 5 halftime performers indicating that their career was positively enhanced by participating in the halftime show if, in actuality, the halftime show had no effect on their career. Since the *p*-value of .1875 is greater than the alpha level of significance (0.01), the null hypothesis is accepted. Based on this limited data, it cannot be confirmed that performing at halftime of the Super Bowl was beneficial to the artists in their future per concert gross revenue.

While statistically we must accept the null hypothesis, there is a great wonder as to whether the same results would be found had the data been available for the 135 concerts that were not included in this data set. Of the available data used, only one artist, Katy Perry, had a decrease in the average gross revenue per show. That decrease was enough to increase the *p*-value of the sign test to a level where the null hypothesis had to be accepted. Overall, with such limited data, an asterisk may be appropriate for the findings concerning concert revenues.

It is interesting to consider why Katy Perry had the decrease in average gross revenue. Her median ticket price fell from $106 to $80, and, as we would expect from the Law of Demand, the average quantity of tickets sold increased from 13,132 per show to 13,415. This would indicate an elasticity of demand of 0.088 for her tickets. With an inelastic demand, lowering the ticket price was not a good strategy for increasing revenue. We know nothing behind the details of the pricing strategies for that tour or if this decrease in price was even under the control of the artist.

Table 5.6 Concert gross revenue sign test results

Variable	*n*	*Sample median*	*Below*	*Equal*	*Above*	*p-value*
Difference in average gross	5	870447	1	0	4	0.1875

The Halftime Show and Additional Income Sources

At first glance it may seem that music consumption and concert revenues are the only areas where a halftime artist could benefit from being associated with the Super Bowl. Executives within the entertainment industry have indicated that there are more areas of revenue to consider. An entertainment attorney who represents a past Super Bowl performer indicated that for stars of the magnitude worthy of consideration for a Super Bowl appearance, less than 20% of their income is generated by recorded music. Concerts, naturally, are important elements of their income, but endorsements can be the second largest segment of their income stream.

With the increased popularity and recognition that comes from a Super Bowl appearance, the asking price in all other areas of income occurs. Endorsements, such as appearing in a commercial can be very lucrative. Since the Super Bowl has an international appeal, the breadth of an advertising campaign featuring the artist increases as well, and along with it the fee for appearing. As a result, the artist can command a fee from $2 million to $10 million per endorsement.

A residency in Las Vegas is a situation where the artist performs a series of concerts at the same location in town, usually at a theatre associated with a major hotel. A successful Super Bowl halftime show can stimulate interest to the point of extending a residency, in one case, by two months. That artist was paid $5 million per month. In order to be able to pay the artist these amounts, the premier tickets for these concerts increased from $250 to $350 per seat following the Super Bowl performance.

In addition, in the days leading up to the Super Bowl, an artist may be hired by a corporation hosting a large party to perform a private concert at their function. A private show can bring with it a fee of $4 million for the artist. Other personal appearance opportunities that do not involve a concert may also present themselves to the artist as well. All in all, it would certainly seem that being the halftime performer at the Super Bowl brings with it numerous opportunities for an artist to increase their revenues.

The NFL as a Mercantilist

Given that performing at the Super Bowl has a significant benefit for the halftime performer, and that the costs for the production of the show are borne by the NFL, a question arises as to just what the benefits are for the NFL in putting on this elaborate and expensive show. As mentioned earlier, the presence of a popular halftime act keeps viewers tuned into the network broadcasting the game. Higher ratings directly benefit the network broadcasting the game, but do not immediately benefit the NFL.

The broadcasting network generates revenues from the sale of the advertising time that runs prior to and immediately following the halftime show. The NFL, however, sees no direct benefit for hosting the halftime show aside from their sponsorship deal with Pepsi. For the league, having high ratings for the game, including halftime, allows the NFL to benefit only when future broadcast rights are sold.

Of note, Pepsi is reported to pay upwards of $7 million to be the halftime sponsor. This amount most likely only covers only a portion of the production costs of the show (Florio 2012). The NFL, however, will not confirm the amount of the Pepsi sponsorship nor the production costs of the show (Quenzel 2019).

There is a way that the NFL could more immediately benefit from the halftime show and generate additional revenues, and that is to act as a mercantilist. Since being the halftime performer is financially beneficial for the artist, the NFL could approach the situation, as would a mercantilist, and demand a payment from the performer for the right to be the halftime act. In doing so, the league would be playing a variation of the dictator game from game theory. The league, being the dictator in the game, would decide how much of a benefit to allow to be passed along to the performer. A rational artist would decide that a partial benefit is better than no benefit at all, and would accept the offer and agree to make a payment to the NFL. Reports in the media indicate that the NFL has considered doing this very thing in the past (Gaines 2014).

Were the NFL to do this, the subsequent question would be, how much would the NFL charge the performer? Using Lady Gaga as an example, her benefit of performing was estimated to be approximately $2.5 million earned on game day plus 7 for music consumption alone. Judging by this total, the NFL could not charge her the full amount of the equivalent advertising value of approximately $135 million and expect her to accept the offer. Her costs would outweigh her benefits. As the dictator, the NFL would need to determine an amount to charge that would lead to an acceptance by the performer. Should the NFL make an offer and have it rejected, the artist would have a payoff of $0. In addition, the league would not only fail to receive a payment from the artist, it would also be stuck trying to find another performer for the game, thus giving them a payoff of $0 as well for this round of negotiations.

Table 5.7 Dictator game payoff table

		Lady Gaga *Accept*	*Reject*
NFL	Charge	\$1 million, \$1.5 million	\$0, \$0
	Don't charge	\$0, \$2.5 million	\$0, \$0

A payoff table for a dictator game played between the NFL and a performer is displayed in Table 5.7. In this game, the estimated benefits for Lady Gaga in 2017 are used. The NFL could have charged her \$1 million for the right to be the halftime performer, leaving her a net benefit of \$1.5 million. Should the league not charge her, her benefit would be the full \$2.5 million. Because \$1.5 million is greater than \$0, she would accept the offer made to her by the dictator and agree to pay the fee. The Nash equilibrium for the game is for the NFL to charge her and for Lady Gaga to accept the invitation to play. So, why has the league decided to forego this revenue and not to charge the artists? There is more than one answer to that question.

One reason why the league has not charged the artist to perform can be partially explained if this dictator game is a part of a larger nested game that involves a third party which affects the payoffs for this game (Tsebelis 1990). In this game, the third party would be the NFL fans. While the league could siphon off, for example, a million dollars or more from some artists, those revenues would have to be weighed against a more valuable commodity for the NFL—its reputation with fans. If the NFL is perceived by its fans to be a greedy league because it charges performers to work, the fans could ultimately lose some interest in NFL games which could reduce their amount of watching or attending games (Boren 2017). Such a loss of fans and viewership would far outweigh the gains from charging a fee to the halftime performer.

In the following game theory table, Table 5.8, the payoffs are illus-

Table 5.8 Nested dictator game payoff table, NFL perspective

		Performer *Accept*	*Reject*
NFL	Charge	6, 8	4, 0
	Don't charge	8, 10	5, 0

trated using a scale of 1–10, with 1 being the worst outcome and 10 being the best. The strategy choices for the NFL are to charge the performer or don't charge the performer. The strategy choices for the performer are to accept the NFL offer or reject the offer. The payoffs to the NFL decrease when they charge performers because of the resulting backlash from fans which offset the gains from the fee taken from the performers. If the performers reject the NFL offer, they receive no payoff and the league must then incur the costs of continuing their search for a halftime artist. As this game is constructed, the dominant strategy for the NFL is don't charge. Accepting the offer is a dominant strategy for the performers. The Nash equilibrium for this game would be for the league to not charge and for the performers to accept that offer. Including the fans into a nested game results in altering the payoffs to the point where the NFL would not pursue the mercantilist notion of charging a fee.

Bargaining Power and the Halftime Performer

There is a different approach we can take to this problem. Economists tend to imagine that trade takes place between equals. Bargaining power doesn't tend to enter the story. But in this instance, that probably isn't entirely accurate. Let's go back to how the elaborate halftime shows began. CBS—the Super Bowl broadcaster—saw their halftime audience vanish to a Fox television show that was far more entertaining than sportscasters rehashing something everyone just saw.

Television networks, though, face a significant problem in keeping that halftime audience. They need a performer that has both mass appeal and who is willing to put together a brief show. The payoff to these shows may seem relatively large to those of us who are non-performers. But the huge talents the NFL wants to hire for these shows are not likely to be impressed by the gains to be made from this show. In sum, the supply of such talents is immensely small.

Consequently, it is not surprising that the bargaining power in this negotiation lies with the performer. The NFL could demand a more equitable split of the revenues but it is likely the NFL lacks the ability to insist on such a split when negotiating with a very limited supply of talent.

Saying No to Halftime

The lack of bargaining power became clear when we consider what happened in 2019. It was reported in 2019 that at least three artists (Jay-Z, Rhianna, and Cardi B) had each been invited to be the halftime performer at the Super Bowl. Each of them turned the offer down (Bowenbank 2018). Assuming that the benefits to the performers for being the halftime act are well known within the entertainment community, there is a question as to why any performer would turn down this opportunity. It would appear that the artist is making a less than rational decision by saying no to the show. It could be, though, that the error being made here is not on the part of the artist, but on the part of the observer. What may seem like a non-optimal strategy choice to the observer may actually be a rational choice by the player (Tsebelis 1990).

The public image of the performer has to be considered as he or she decides whether to accept the invitation to perform at the Super Bowl.[1] The artists who reportedly turned down the 2019 invitations may have done so in order to show solidarity with former NFL player Colin Kaepernick. Kaepernick had been criticized for kneeling in protest during the playing of the national anthem prior to NFL games during the 2016 season (Bowenbank 2018). When Kaepernick became a free agent in the spring of 2017, he did not receive any offers from NFL teams. Many felt that Kaepernick had been blackballed by league teams for expressing his protest against police brutality and racial inequality (Bowenbank 2018). By performing at the halftime show, these artists could potentially see a decline in demand from their fans who were also in support of Kaepernick. The artists' concern was that their fans would view a performance at the Super Bowl as being detrimental to their political cause. This could result in fans turning their backs on the artists and decreasing both their music consumption and concert attendance.

The game theory table in Table 5.9 shows the payoffs to the NFL and to the performer if fans dislike the artist for agreeing to be the halftime performer and being viewed as supporting the policies of the NFL. The payoffs are hypothesized and are on a scale of 1–10, with 10 being the

[1] We also should at least acknowledge that the performers are motivated by something other than monetary issues. The performers may not have just been motivated by what might happen to their public image. They might have also been protesting how the NFL handled the Kaepernick case in the past.

Table 5.9 Nested dictator game payoff table, artist perspective

		Performer	
		Accept	*Reject*
NFL	Charge	6, 4	4, 7
	Don't charge	8, 5	5, 7

best outcome. The payoff to the performer reflects the fans disapproval and therefore results in lower payoffs than shown in Table 5.8. If the artist is correct in their assessment of this game, then being the halftime performer would result in lower payoffs. This concern with lower payoffs results in the artist rejecting the invitation to perform. Rejecting the offer is a dominant strategy. The Nash equilibrium for this game is for the NFL not to charge and for the artist to reject. The seemingly irrational decision to reject the offer can be now understood to indeed be a rational choice on the part of the artist.

Rather than perform at the Super Bowl, Cardi B and Bruno Mars instead held a concert at State Farm Arena in Atlanta, the city hosting the 2019 Super Bowl, the Saturday prior to the game. Their fans responded by buying 14,152 tickets for that show, which set a venue record of $6.5 million in ticket sales (Brooks 2019).

Despite the controversy, Maroon 5 did agree to be that year's halftime performer. Doing so did not detract from the benefits they received from their fan base by being the halftime performer. Maroon 5 reportedly saw a 587% increase in music sold from the day before the game to the day of the game (Caulfield 2019).

A Brief History of NFL Cheerleaders

The NFL appears to lack bargaining power when it negotiates with halftime performers. It is a very different story when we turn to NFL cheerleaders. Before we get to the story of bargaining power in the market for NFL cheerleaders we need to review some history. Historically the NFL has been a male dominated venture. The original owners in 1920 were all men.[2] The coaches and referees were men. The media covering the games were men. And of course, all the players were men.

One hundred years later the story has changed. Today, six of the NFL's 32 franchises are owned by women. Another four franchises are co-owned by women.[3] Women are also frequently hired as team executives. Amy Trask became the first chief executive officer when she assumed this position for the Oakland Raiders in 1997 and[4] the current majority of executives with the Philadelphia Eagles are also women. Across the NFL, 28% of all NFL employees are women, although that percentage drops to 18% when we consider positions at the level of vice president or higher.[5]

Women have also made in-roads with respect to what happens on the field. In 2015, Sarah Thomas became the first woman to be hired as a referee (Fox 2015). The next year, Kathryn Smith became the first woman to be hired full-time as a coach when the Buffalo Bills put her in charge of quality control. By 2019, five more women had also been hired as coaches by NFL teams (Rutter 2020). As of yet, women haven't been hired to play the game.[6] But women are increasingly part of the NFL.

As noted, this is quite the change from what we have seen in the past. Historically the only role women really had in football was that of cheerleader. And the most of famous of these has been the Dallas Cowboys Cheerleaders.

Once again, the NFL Super Bowl halftime spectacular was born out of a need in 1992 to keep an audience tuned to the same station

[2] The first woman to own an NFL team was Violet Bidwell-Wolfner. She inherited the Chicago Cardinals from her husband when he passed away in 1947 (see https://thebigredzone.com/2020/01/10/remembering-violet-bidwill-wolfner-first-female-nfl-owner/). Georgia Frontiere became the second woman to own an NFL team when she inherited the Los Angeles Rams in 1979 (Altavilla 2000). Oddly enough, both women inherited teams that they later moved to St. Louis.

[3] The identity of NFL owners in 2020 can be found here: https://www.yardbarker.com/nfl/articles/nfl_owners_from_oldest_to_youngest/s1__29789828#slide_1.

[4] Source: https://www.nfl.com/photos/influential-women-in-football-0ap3000000812590.

[5] Beaton (2019) also notes that 23 of the NFL's 32 teams has at least one woman working in a vice president position or higher in the organization.

[6] Women have played college football. Katie Hnida was the first woman to play in a college football game when she attempted an extra point in 2002. The next year she became the first woman to score in a Division-I football games. https://www.history.com/this-day-in-history/katie-hnida-is-first-woman-to-play-in-division-i-football-game.

broadcasting the Super Bowl when the game wasn't being played. This problem, though, didn't suddenly appear in the early 1990s. In fact, this basic issue led Tex Schramm—general manager of the Dallas Cowboys—to create perhaps the most famous performing group in football history.

An average NFL game has an immense amount of downtime. A typical NFL broadcast lasts more than three hours. The actual game—as judged by the game clock—is 60 minutes. But when we look at actual game action—as Seward (2013) notes—a typical game only gives its viewers about 11 minutes worth of football to watch.

It turns out a typical NFL game is a middle-manager's dream. Yes, most of the broadcast consists of just meetings. There are meetings between players (i.e., huddles before each play). There are also meetings between coaches and players. But that's not all. The coaches meet by themselves and also with the referees. The referees themselves also hold meetings. We are not aware of exactly how many meetings happen during a typical NFL game, but the number has to be in triple digits. Although people love watching actual football, it turns out few people—except maybe dedicated middle-managers—really love watching meetings.

As Dana Adam Shapiro noted (Ruiz 2018), this issue essentially led Schramm to create the Dallas Cowboys Cheerleaders:

> "Schramm was known as the P. T. Barnum of the NFL," says Dana Adam Shapiro, director of Daughters of the Sexual Revolution: The Untold Story of the Dallas Cowboys Cheerleaders. "He was the one who had the initial vision for showgirls on the sidelines of sporting events. He realized there's a lot of downtime in football. It couldn't just be guys on the field running into each other. You had to turn it into showbiz. And the cheerleaders were one of the ways that he turned it into the greatest show on earth."

As Lurie (2014) tells the story, Schramm implemented his vision in 1972.

> (Schramm) hires choreographer Texie Waterman in 1972 and, soon after, director Suzanne Mitchell. Under their lead, cheerleading becomes a tantalizing dance: Women perform choreographed routines in short shorts and midriff-bearing uniforms.

It is important to emphasize that Schramm did not invent the concept of cheerleaders at football games in 1972. The history of cheerleaders goes back to the nineteenth century.

As Ruiz (2018) notes:

> In the beginning, cheerleaders were neither modest women nor sexy women. In fact, they weren't women at all. As college football took off in the early 1900s, enthusiastic male students in the then all-male Ivy League organically spilled out of the stands and onto the sidelines, becoming the first "yell leaders" and "rooter kings." Perhaps not coincidentally, when cheerleading was a predominantly male activity, it carried considerably more weight. "The reputation of having been a valiant 'cheer-leader' is one of the most valuable things a boy can take away from college," The Nation wrote in 1911.

By 1940, there were more than 30,000 cheerleading teams in high schools and colleges around the country (Lurie 2014). But when those cheerleaders (again, they were mostly men)[7] went off to fight World War II, women—as they did with many jobs at the time—took over (Ruiz 2018).

In 1954, the Baltimore Colts became the first NFL team to hire cheerleaders (Ruiz 2018). Well, hire is not quite the correct term. As Ruiz (2018) reports, these first cheerleaders weren't paid at all.

Life was quite different for the Dallas Cowboys Cheerleaders. They most definitely got paid. As Ruiz (2018) reports:

> (The Dallas Cowboys Cheerleaders) were paid around $100 per season, before taxes—barely enough to cover gas to the stadium and dry cleaning for their iconic uniforms. As one former cheerleader told filmmaker Dana Adam Shapiro, "We became million-dollar showgirls who made $15 a game."

Million-dollar showgirls is not an exaggeration. In 1976, free-lance photographer Bob Shaw was hired to photograph five cheerleaders for a poster.[8] The poster turned out to be immensely successful. Shaw was only paid $14,000 for the shoot. But the Cowboys earned $1.8 million from the poster. As for the cheerleaders... well, Shaw confessed he paid them nothing.

This was not the last time the most famous cheerleaders in America were paid nothing. The 1978 Super Bowl was contended between the Dallas Cowboys and the Denver Broncos. Of course, the Cowboys were

[7] Ninemire (2019) reports that women didn't start participating in cheerleading until 1923.

[8] The story of this poster is told in Ruiz (2018).

not just content to bring their team. The cheerleaders were also asked to come and perform.

Debbie Kepley—who was a Dallas Cowboy Cheerleader from 1976 to 1978—noted she wasn't paid anything for performing at the Super Bowl (Ruiz 2018): "*These guys get these $10,000 rings and these big bonuses, and they couldn't even give us our $14.12.*"[9]

What Is an NFL Cheerleader Worth?

In the twenty-first century, pay had not changed dramatically. In 2014, a woman identified as Laci T. brought a lawsuit against the Oakland Raiders. The lawsuit alleged that the Raiders…

> …(failed) to pay its Raiderettes (the team's cheerleaders) minimum wage, withholds their pay until the end of the season, imposes illegal fines for minor infractions (like gaining 5 pounds), and forces cheerleaders to pay their own business expenses (everything from false eyelashes to monthly salon visits).[10]

As a result of this lawsuit, it was reported (Breech 2014) that each cheerleader who was with the Raiderettes would receive $6400 for each season they performed. In addition, going forward the cheerleaders were guaranteed $9 an hour. This was the minimum wage in the state of California at this time.[11] Yes, the cheerleaders had to go to court just to make sure they were getting paid the same as a new hire at Burger King.

One should note that this lawsuit didn't apply to all cheerleaders. Berri (2016) looked at what it would mean if all NFL cheerleaders were guaranteed the federal minimum wage. According to this article, a typical NFL cheerleader works about 11 hours per week across a 20-week NFL season. With a federal minimum wage of $7.25, that works out to $1595 per year. Although that doesn't sound like much, it is much better than what the Cowboys were paying their cheerleaders in 1977. At that time the federal minimum wage was $2.30.[12] If these cheerleaders worked as much as

[9] An NFL team only played seven home games at this time. The $14.12 refers to what each cheerleader received for each home game after taxes.

[10] Hess (2014).

[11] Source: https://www.dir.ca.gov/iwc/minimumwagehistory.htm.

[12] https://www.dol.gov/agencies/whd/minimum-wage/history/chart.

their counterparts today, they would have been paid about $500 for a season.[13] Once again, though, these cheerleaders were only paid $100 for the season (this is about $420 in 2019 dollars).[14]

In sum, once again cheerleaders today are being paid as well as a new fast food hire. The famous Dallas Cowboys Cheerleaders from the 1970s were paid about 20–25% of that pay! All of this leads us to ask, what is a cheerleader worth? Berri (2016) notes there are three ways NFL cheerleaders generate revenue:

The Honey Shot.

Andy Sidaris—director of ABC's Monday Night Football in the 1970s—invented what became known as the "honey shot."[15] Once again, an NFL game is mostly a series of meetings. Sidaris would routinely cut away from the meetings to show the cheerleaders on the sideline. As Sidaris admitted: "I got the idea for honey shots because I am a dirty old man," yes, exploitation of cheerleaders goes well beyond the issue of economics.[16]

Of course, Sidaris and other television directors were not the only people seeking to exploit the cheerleaders with respect to these television appearances. Boudway (2014) reported how much time on television was worth. According to the research of two students (Molly Cosby and Sehrish Sohel),[17] the average cheerleader in 2015 appeared on air for ten seconds per game. Given the numbers noted by Boudway (2014), this means an average NFL cheerleader squad generated $450,000 per year just from their brief television appearances.

[13] 11 hours per week for 20 weeks is 220 hours. At $2.30 per hour, that works out to $506.

[14] Cheerleader pay was converted into real 2019 dollars via the data on the Consumer Price Index reported by the Minneapolis Federal Reserve: https://www.minneapolisfed.org/community/financial-and-economic-education/cpi-calculator-information/consumer-price-index-and-inflation-rates-1913.

[15] The story of Sidaris and the "honey shot" is told by Ruiz (2018).

[16] Cheerleaders have also faced more than just economic exploitation. The most recent example was reported in the Washington Post in August of 2020. In this story (Schad 2020) it was alleged that someone compiled what were described a "lewd outtakes" from videos taken of the team's cheerleaders. Other instances of sexual harassment were also alleged.

[17] The work of Cosby and Sohel was reported in Berri (2016).

How much of this revenue should go to the individual cheerleaders? The NFL shares 48% of its revenue with its players. If the NFL did this with its cheerleaders, the NFL would be giving $216,000 to each squad. And with an average of 32 members per team, each woman would receive $6750. Of course, the cheerleaders didn't receive this money. So, the exploitation went far beyond the bad behavior of Sidaris and other people in television.

Value of Performing

Obviously, the time the cheerleaders spend on television is a very small part of the time they spend doing their job. The primary job these cheerleaders are hired to do is dance at game. What is the value of this activity?

Only six teams in the NFL in 2019 did not have official cheerleaders.[18] We could look at how team revenue is impacted by having a cheerleading team. However—as we note in our discussion of the economic value of quarterbacks—more than 60% of team revenue is shared in the NFL. Consequently, team revenue doesn't appear to be impacted by team wins. It certainly isn't going to be impacted by having cheerleaders dance on the sideline.

Of course, the players' performance on the field does have value to the teams. And we tend to think the cheerleaders also have value. Berri (2016) offered a way to think about that value. Essentially cheerleaders are hired as dancers. As Berri (2016) reported, dancers in Broadway musicals are paid a minimum of $1917 per week. If someone dances in a regional theater, weekly pay ranges from $560 to $730 per week. Dancers in these shows, though, likely work 40 hours per week while NFL cheerleaders do not. Therefore, we need to consider a dancer's hourly wage to determine what cheerleaders should be paid for their dancing.

For a Broadway dancer, the minimum hourly wage is $47.93 per hour. For the lowest paid regional theater dancers, that minimum wage is $14 per hour. Given the NFL cheerleaders schedule of 11 hours per week for 20 weeks, the wage for dancing for the entire season would range

[18] These six are the Buffalo Bills, Chicago Bears, Cleveland Browns, Green Bay Packers, the New York Giants, and the Pittsburgh Steelers. The Bills had a cheerleading squad until 2013. After the cheerleaders filed a lawsuit over their working conditions the team was disbanded (O'Shei and Liu 2019).

from $3080 to $10,500. Yes, both numbers are far beyond the wage they receive when they are paid like a minimum wage hire at a fast food chain.

Promotional Appearances

NFL cheerleaders don't just perform at games. They are often asked to work at other events. In 2014 the Buffalo Bills cheerleader filed a lawsuit against the team alleging that the cheerleaders were asked to do quite a bit of additional unpaid work. As Hess (2014) reported, the cheerleaders were asked to

> … (parade) around casinos in bikinis "for the gratification of the predominantly male crowd"; and offering themselves up as prizes at a golf tournament, where they were required to sit on men's laps on the golf carts, submerge themselves in a dunk tank, and perform backflips for tips (which they did not receive).

Once again, cheerleaders were not just exploited economically. We should also note, not all teams fail to pay their cheerleaders for these events. Lisa Murray—a former dancer with the Golden State Warriors and a cheerleader activist noted[19] that the San Francisco 49ers receive $300 per hour for each cheerleader at an event and the team gives $175 of that money to the cheerleader. Each event lasts a minimum of two hours, and Murray argues it is possible a cheerleader could do about 20 events per year. Therefore, it is possible a cheerleader with the 49ers earned about $7000 per year from promotional events.

Let's imagine all cheerleaders were paid

- for each of the brief television appearances
- like a professional dancer
- like the 49ers pay for promotional appearances

then each cheerleader would be paid between $16,830 and $24,250 per year. Of course, those numbers are ignoring what cheerleaders could be paid for calendars, posters, videos, merchandise, etc. But even if we put those issues aside, cheerleaders who are only paid a minimum wage and who are not paid for promotional appearances are dramatically underpaid.

[19] Lisa Murray's discussion of promotional events was reported in Berri (2016).

So, why are cheerleaders so poorly paid? According to Ninemire (2019), there are 3.4 million cheerleaders in the United States (age 13 years old and older) and the majority of these are female.[20] So, there are a large number of women who have some cheerleading experience. But there are clearly very limited opportunities to do this professionally. When supply greatly exceeds demand, prices tend to fall.

In addition, many cheerleaders report they are very happy with their cheerleading experience and are not at all sympathetic with the women who brought lawsuits against teams. As Loren Kuwik—former co-captain of the Buffalo Bills cheerleaders—argued[21]:

> If you had such a problem volunteering your time, just because you weren't being compensated for it, then why were you there? Get a paid dancing job somewhere.

As Kuwik argues, the cheerleaders knew what the compensation would be before they started. And since one can argue that compensation simply reflects supply and demand, what is the problem?

As Berri (2018) notes, the economist Joan Robinson defined exploitation as a worker's economic value being more than the worker's wage. A worker's economic value—or what economists call Marginal Revenue Product—is about how much revenue a worker produces for the firm. Nowhere in the definition does one consider whether the worker is happy with their job or whether the supply of workers is responsible for depressing their wages.

Perhaps a brief discussion of baseball history is instructive. Baseball introduced veteran player free agency in 1976. Berri and Krautmann (2019) report prior to free agency, pay for Major League Baseball players was quite low. For example, baseball in 1953 only paid about 20% of its revenue to its players. This study also reports a similar result for the New York Yankees—a team that featured such legends as Babe Ruth and Lou Gehrig—in the 1920s.

[20] It should be noted that cheerleading in high school and college is not a low-risk activity. Kimberly Archie is a cheerleading activist. She notes that 70% of catastrophic injuries to female athletes in college are sustained by cheerleaders.

[21] Tim O'Shei and Qina Liu. (2019).

Were baseball players unhappy? Well, they all certainly volunteered to play baseball for Major League Baseball. And we have this quote[22] from 1964 that suggests some players were quite satisfied with how baseball was operated before free agency.

> In 1964 Judge Robert Cannon, a lawyer representing the Major League Baseball Player Association (MLBPA), offered this insight into the plight of the American athlete. Testifying before the U.S. Senate, Cannon observed: "If I might, Senator, preface my remarks by repeating the words of Gene Woodling ... 'we have it so good we don't know what to ask for next.' I think this sums up the thinking of the average major league ballplayer today."

So, does this mean baseball players were not exploited before free agency? As Adshade and Berri (2015) observe:

> Worker exploitation has nothing to do with how much someone likes their job, or how much that job improves a worker's other prospects, or whether or not the job can help her fulfill other life goals.

This needs to be remembered when we talk about exploitation in sports. It is true when we talk about baseball players before free agency, college athletes, or cheerleaders. Whether or not those individuals are happy or not, is not relevant to the argument that they are being exploited.

Conclusion

The story of the NFL and the performers it hired often comes down to bargaining power. Maintaining the TV audience during halftime of the Super Bowl game is important enough to the NFL that the league chooses to absorb the costs of producing an elaborate show. The headlining entertainers who perform at the show are barely compensated by the league for doing so. Instead, their appearance serves as an advertisement for their music. A sign test was performed on pre and postgame data on weighted song consumption of music by those artists for the 2014 through 2017 Super Bowls. The results were significant at the .01 level, indicating that appearing as the halftime performer provides a

[22] This was reported in Berri et al. (2006).

significant boost in music consumption for those artists. During this time period, artists saw, on average, an increase in marginal revenue for music consumption of $117,571 per day for game day and for the seven days following the game.

While it would seem logical that similar benefits would be seen for concert performances following the Super Bowl, the limited data set used did not show a significant increase. Despite showing, on average, a marginal revenue increase of $845,270 in gross concert revenue, the number of shows which had to be excluded from the data set limited the ability to statistically confirm this benefit. Future researchers with better access to data are left to examine this area more fully.

The question as to why the NFL does not seek to capture some of the producer surplus by charging the artists to perform at halftime was examined. Two possibilities were considered. First, we considered the idea the NFL was motivated by people's perceptions of its behavior. If the league believes that charging performers will alienate fans, the revenue gained from the artists would be more than offset by the loss of ticket sales and viewers. A decrease in those areas would spill over into a loss of sponsorship and broadcasting dollars. The league's behavior indicates that it believes it is better off letting the artist gain from the halftime show, keeping fans entertained and tuned in, and protecting the popularity of the league.

Another possibility, though, is that the NFL faces a significant problem negotiating with a very limited supply of marquee halftime performers. The NFL needs a major star to keep its halftime audience. There simply aren't that many performers with enough mass appeal to keep that audience.

The issue of bargaining power is further illustrated by how the NFL has treated its cheerleaders. The NFL seems to face a limited supply of marquee stars for its halftime show but when it comes to the market for NFL cheerleaders, the labor supply greatly exceeds the NFL's demand. Consequently, the pay of cheerleaders has historically been immensely depressed and the NFL has been able to exploit this talent. And yes—as we noted—exploitation still exists even if a person likes their job!

The story of the performers at the Super Bowl highlights how differences in bargaining power can often play a huge role in the outcomes we observe. When the NFL doesn't have much bargaining power it finds that its deal with the performers is—from the NFL's perspective—relatively bad. But when the NFL has bargaining power… well, the story of the NFL cheerleaders tells us the NFL is not afraid to exploit the power it possesses in the marketplace.

References

Adshade, M., & Berri, D. (2015, March 25). Pay Cheerleaders What They're Worth. *Time*. Retrieved from http://time.com/3752957/nfl-football-cheerleaders-minimum-wage/.

Allen, B. (2018, April 19). Bruno Mars' 24K Magic Tour Earns $240 Million (So Far). *Billboard*. Retrieved from https://www.billboard.com/articles/columns/chart-beat/8356825/bruno-mars-24k-magic-tour-earnings.

Altavilla, J. (2000, January 27). When "One of the Boys" Is a Woman. *Hartford Courant*. Retrieved from https://www.courant.com/news/connecticut/hc-xpm-2000–01-27-0001270029-story.html.

Anderson, D. R., Sweeney, D. J., & Williams, T. A. (1999). *Statistics for Business and Economics*. Cincinnati, OH: South-Western College Publishing.

Beaton, A. (2019, September 25). The NFL Team Run by Women. *Wall Street Journal*. https://www.wsj.com/articles/the-nfl-team-run-by-women-11569412442.

Berri, D. (2016, June 8). Why Sports Cheerleaders and Dancers Are Worth More Than Minimum Wage. *Vice Sports*. Retrieved from https://sports.vice.com/en_us/article/why-sports-cheerleaders-and-dancers-are-worth-more-than-minimum-wage.

Berri, D. (2018, May). *Sports Economics*. New York, NY: Worth Publishers/Macmillan Education.

Berri, D. J., & Krautmann, A. C. (2019). How Much did Baseball's Antitrust Exemption Cost Bob Gibson? *The Antitrust Bulletin, 64*(4), 566–583.

Berri, D., Schmidt, M., & Brook, S. (2006). *The Wages of Wins: Taking Measure of the Many Myths in Modern Sport*. Stanford University Press.

Boren, C. (2017, October 26). Mark Cuban Foresaw an NFL 'Implosion' of Greed. Now, He says, It's 'Accelerating.' *The Washington Post*. Retrieved from https://www.washingtonpost.com/news/early-lead/wp/2017/10/26/mark-cuban-foresaw-an-nfl-implosion-of-greed-now-he-says-its-accelerating/?noredirect=on&utm_term=.3ccecc555230.

Boudway, I. (2014, September 11). What Are NFL Cheerleaders Worth? Insider Their Fight for Minimum Wage. *Bloomberg Businessweek*. Retrieved from https://www.bloomberg.com/news/articles/2014-09-10/nfl-cheerleaders-battle-teams-for-minimum-wage.

Bowenbank, S. (2018, October 22). 5 Artists Who Reportedly Turned Down Super Bowl Halftime Show. *Billboard*. Retrieved from https://www.billboard.com/articles/news/super-bowl/8481199/rihanna-musicians-turned-down-super-bowl-halftime-show.

Breech, J. (2014, September 4). Cheerleaders Reach $1.25 Million Settlement in Lawsuit Against Raiders. *CBS Sports*. Retrieved from https://www.cbssports.com/nfl/news/cheerleaders-reach-125-million-settlement-in-lawsuit-against-raiders/.

Brooks, D. (2019, March 23). Behind the Boxscore: Supersized Grosses. *Billboard, 131,* 7, 72.

BuzzAngle Music 2017 U.S. Report. (2017). A Report on 2017 U.S. Music Industry Consumption. *BuzzAngle Music*. Retrieved from http://buzzanglemusic.com.

Cassels, C. (2018, September 26). Super Exposure for Super Bowl Halftime. *Auxoro*. Retrieved from https://www.auxoro.com/hustle/2018/9/25/super-exposure-for-super-bowl-halftime.

Caulfield, K. (2019, February 2). Maroon 5 Super Bowl Halftime Show Yields 434% Sales Gain in U.S. *Billboard*. Retrieved from https://www.billboard.com/articles/columns/chart-beat/8496316/maroon-5-super-bowl-halftime-show-sales-gain-spongebob-travis-scott-big-boi?utm_source=Sailthru&utm_medium=email&utm_campaign=Newsletter%20Template%20BB:%20Single%20Story%20-%201.0&utm_term=biz_breakingnews.

Christman, E. (2019, May 9). Rolling Stone Magazine to Launch Music Charts. *Billboard*. Retrieved from https://www.billboard.com/articles/business/8510461/rolling-stone-magazine-music-charts.

Florio, M. (2012, June 25). Pepsi Returns as Super Bowl Halftime Sponsor. *NBC Sports*. Retrieved from https://profootballtalk.nbcsports.com/2012/06/25/pepsi-returns-as-super-bowl-halftime-sponsor/.

Fox, A. (2015, April 17). Meet Sarah Thomas, NFL's First Female Official. *ESPN*. Retrieved from https://www.espn.com/nfl/story/_/id/12669370/meet-sarah-thomas-first-female-nfl-official-referee.

Gaines, C. (2014, August 22). Why the NFL Charging Artists to Perform at Halftime of the Super Bowl Is a Genius Move. *Business Insider*. Retrieved from https://www.businessinsider.com/nfl-artists-super-bowl-halftime-2014-8.

Hartmann, W. R., & Klapper, D. (2017). Super Bowl Ads. *Marketing Science, 37*(1), 78–96.

Hess, A. (2014, April 23). The Cheerleaders Rise Up. *Slate*. Retrieved from https://slate.com/human-interest/2014/04/nfl-cheerleading-lawsuits-five-former-buffalo-jills-are-the-latest-in-a-string-of-cheerleaders-to-sue-their-teams.html.

History.com Editors. (2019, December 20). Katie Hnida Is First Woman to Play in Division I Football Game. *History*. A&E Publishers. Retrieved from https://www.history.com/this-day-in-history/katie-hnida-is-first-woman-to-play-in-division-i-football-game.

Johnson, B. (2017, January 10). Super Bowl in Game Ad Spending: Average Cost for :30 Second Spot. *Ad Age*. Retrieved from https://adage.com/

article/special-report-super-bowl/super-bowl-supersized-4-9-billion-ad-spending-51-years/307361/.
Johnson, M. (2020, March 3). NFL Says 47 Percent of Fans Are Women, Launches Women's History Month. *Yardbarker.* Retrieved from https://www.msn.com/en-us/sports/nfl/nfl-says-47-percent-of-fans-are-women-launches-women-s-history-month/ar-BB10EvUf.
Katz, F. (2018, June 12). The Guide to Music Streaming Platforms. *Songtrust.* Retrieved from https://blog.songtrust.com/the-guide-to-music-streaming-platforms.
Krueger, A. B. (2019). *Rockonomics: A Backstage Tour of What the Music Industry Can Teach Us About Economics and Life.* New York, NY: Currency Press.
Ku, R. S. R. (2002). The Creative Destruction of Copyright: Napster and the New Economics of Digital Technology. *The University of Chicago Law Review, 69*(1), 263–324.
Lurie, J. (2014, December 15). A Not-So-Brief and Extremely Sordid History of Cheerleading. *Mother Jones.* Retrieved from https://www.motherjones.com/media/2014/12/cheerleader-history-timeline/.
Newman, M. (2019, February 1). Why Isn't the Super Bowl Halftime Show Ready for Some Country? *Billboard.* Retrieved from https://www.billboard.com/articles/news/super-bowl/8496109/super-bowl-halftime-show-country-music-headliners?utm_source=Sailthru&utm_medium=email&utm_campaign=Newsletter%20Template%20BB:%20Multi%20Story%20-%201.0&utm_term=daily_digest.
Nielsen NPM. (2018). *Super Bowl Ratings: Live Plus Same Day.* The Nielsen Company.
Ninemire, V. (2019, January 4). Cheerleading Fun Facts & History. *LiveAbout.* Retrieved from https://www.liveabout.com/cheerleading-history-4080643.
Osborne, M. J., & Rubinstein, A. (1994). *A Course in Game Theory.* Cambridge: MIT Press.
O'Shei, T., & Qina, L. (2019, June 18). Could the Buffalo Bills Get Cheerleaders Again? *The Buffalo News.* Retrieved from https://buffalonews.com/sports/bills/could-the-buffalo-bills-get-cheerleaders-again/article_1bbabaaa-f11f-5b59-bff2-7d56b8e1e2be.html.
Quenzel, M. (2019, February 20). Personal Communication.
Raithela, S., Taylor, C. R., & Hock, S. J. (2016). Are Super Bowl Ads a Super Waste of Money? Examining the Intermediary Roles of Customer-Based Brand Equity and Customer Equity Effects. *Journal of Business Research, 69*(9), 3788–3794.
Ruiz, M. (2018, October 4). Sex on the Sidelines: How the NFL Made a Game of Exploiting Cheerleaders. *Vanity Fair.* Retrieved from https://www.vanityfair.com/style/2018/10/nfl-cheerleaders-history-scandal.

Rutter, J. (2020, February 1). Planting Seeds: Women Look to Grow Ranks as NFL Coaches. *Tribune-Review*. Retrieved from https://triblive.com/sports/planting-seeds-women-look-to-grow-ranks-as-nfl-coaches/.

SAG-AFTRA. (2018). *SAG-AFTRA Television Agreement Wage Tables*. Retrieved from https://www.sagaftra.org/production-center/contract/810/rate-sheet/document.

Sanchez, D. (2018, March 29). Apple Music, Not Spotify, Ranks as the Most Popular Music Streaming Service. *Digital Music News*. Retrieved from https://www.digitalmusicnews.com/2018/03/29/verto-analytics-study-apple-music-spotify/.

Schad, T. (2020, August 26). Washington Football Team Compiled Lewd Video Outtakes of Cheerleaders, Per Report. *USA Today*. Retrieved from https://www.usatoday.com/story/sports/nfl/washington/2020/08/26/dan-snyder-washington-football-team-cheerleader-video-outtakes-sexual-harassment/3443158001/.

Seward, Z. (2013, November 24). An Average NFL Game: More Than 100 Commercials and Just 11 Minutes of Play. *Quartz*. Retrieved from https://qz.com/150577/an-average-nfl-game-more-than-100-commercials-and-just-11-minutes-of-play/.

Sports Illustrated. (2017, February 3). Who Has Performed at Super Bowl Halftime? *SI Wire*. Retrieved from https://www.si.com/nfl/2017/02/05/super-bowl-halftime-performances.

Songcast. (2019). Learn How to Get Your Music on iTunes and Collect Royalties. *Songcast*. Retrieved from https://www.songcastmusic.com/faq/learn-how-to-get-your-music-on-itunes-and-collect-royalties.

Super Bowl Ratings History. (2020). *Sports Media Watch*. Retrieved from https://www.sportsmediawatch.com/super-bowl-ratings-historical-viewership-chart-cbs-nbc-fox-abc/.

Tsebelis, G. (1990). *Nested Games: Rational Choice in Comparative Politics*. Berkeley: University of California Press.

CHAPTER 6

Summary and Conclusions

Abstract Ex ante economic impact studies of the Super Bowl show that the presence of the game in a city does not provide the level of economic benefit that proponents of the game claim it has. Halftime performers appear to perform in order to gain expose for their music. Their performance results in significantly higher levels of music consumption. The impact their appearance has on future concert ticket sales is in need of further research. Quarterbacks who win the Super Bowl see a benefit of around $2 million in their future playing contracts. Measuring the marginal revenue product of quarterbacks is difficult because it is interrelated with other players in this team sport.

Keywords Economic impact studies · Music consumption · Pay inequality · Quarterback rating · Marginal revenue product

The purpose of this book was to give a brief history of the championship game of the NFL, and to explore the size and scope of three particular aspects of the Super Bowl with an in-depth look at those distinct elements that are affected by the game. The focus was threefold, the cities that host the game, the players who participate in the game, and the performers at the game.

Y. J. Kelly et al., *The Economics of the Super Bowl*, Palgrave Pivots in Sports Economics, https://doi.org/10.1007/978-3-030-46370-0_6

Of the three areas covered in this book, the economic impact of mega-events has been the most previously studied. In fact, one might argue the Super Bowl's biggest impact is on the academic careers of those investigating its impact. This work adds to the literature by updating and refining previous theories and findings. Ex ante economic impact estimates were found to be overstatements of what ex post economic impact studies actually found took place. In looking at the non-monetary benefits of hosting, several limitations were discussed which imply a decreasing marginal benefit of the publicity generated for the host city. It becomes clear that the awarding of the Super Bowl is an enticement to cities and has been used to extract public funding for new stadiums or extensive renovations. Ex ante NFL estimates of the economic impact for the host city were ten times greater than the ex post benefits actually received by these cities.

Given this incentive by the supporters of the game to overstate the benefits received by the host cities, several areas of concern in their economic analysis were presented. The crowding out effect where visitors to a city are replaced by Super Bowl attendees; the substitution effect, where locals choose the event over another local activity; leakages, where spending in the local economy does not remain in the area measured by the study; casual visitors, those who did not come to the town particularly for the game but ended up attending anyway; and time switchers, where guests altered their time to visit in order to coincide with the event, were discussed. The result of not considering these limitations is an overstatement of the financial impact for the city hosting.

The Super Bowl doesn't appear to have much impact for the cities hosting the event. When we turn to the teams, we see a similar story. Because the NFL shares so much revenue, winning games doesn't seem to impact a team's revenue. Winning the Super Bowl seems to have some value, but relative to the revenues a team earns the impact is very small.

It is possible a substantial percentage of what the team receives from winning the Super Bowl is given to the quarterback. Quarterbacks are considered the "face of the franchise" and are given credit for winning games. It appears that teams increase the future pay of quarterbacks who happen to be on the winning side of the Super Bowl. Perhaps surprisingly, though, those winning quarterbacks are not often the very best quarterbacks in the regular season. In other words, your team doesn't need the superior quarterback to end up on the winning side of the NFL's championship game.

An effort was made to put into context what teams appeared to pay the winning quarterbacks. That exploration led us to explore the broader questions: What is the economic value of a player in a team sport? We began by rejecting the standard approach pioneered by Scully (1974). The approach offered by Berri-Goff, though, also appeared to have problems. In the end, we have to acknowledge that in a sport where most everything that happens on the field requires the input of several players, it may not be possible to assign a specific value to each individual.

The last participants we considered were the performers at the Super Bowl who are not on the teams. Both the halftime performers and the cheerleaders entertain the audiences watching the game. We found that the former is able to receive substantial benefits from their appearance while the latter is barely compensated. The reason for both outcomes is the same. The bargaining power of those negotiating with the NFL appears to drive what they receive.

Consider the benefits received by the halftime performer. The affect that being the halftime performer at the Super Bowl has on the career of artists has not been previously examined in the literature. This book is an introduction to this new area and leaves many questions open for future research. Examining the halftime show also blends together two previously distinct areas of study—sports economics and entertainment economics. It can be debated as to whether professional sport is actually a sub-set of the entertainment industry or whether sport is a unique field unto itself.

The Super Bowl halftime show is a very expensive production. Insiders have indicated that the 12-minute show can cost upwards of $25 million in production costs, all borne by the NFL. As it turns out, paying the headlining act is one of the least expensive of those costs. The artists, in essence, volunteer their time to be the halftime performer.

In examining why a premier artist would volunteer their time and effort to appear in the halftime show, and examination of the affect this appearance has on future earnings was undertaken. Data was located identifying eight halftime artists and the consumption of their music the week prior to their Super Bowl appearance, the day of the game, and the week following the game. Using a sign test, it was shown that a statistically significant bump exists in the revenues generated from music consumption following the halftime performance.

Estimates were made concerning the value of this bump in music consumption. A confounding issue is that music is consumed in different formats. Music can be purchased, streamed, or viewed in a music video format. Each of these methods pays the artists a different amount. Even within the category of streaming there are different amounts being paid depending on which streaming service is involved. Thus, estimating value is exactly that—a mere estimate.

The data was unpacked using industry averages and estimates were made concerning the dollar value of the increase in music consumption. For the eight artists included in the study, the average increase for the week following the game was found to average $1,008,041 per artist. Not all artists benefitted equally though, Lady Gaga saw an increase of roughly $2.5 million while the Red Hot Chili Peppers saw an increase of only $69,169. Still, in terms of music consumption, every artist benefitted from performing at the Super Bowl.

Musical artists generate revenue from more sources than just music consumption. Concerts are an important source of income for them. A study of concert revenue data was attempted by comparing average gross concert revenues per artist for the year prior to their Super Bowl appearance to the year following the game. The data here became even more problematic. Some artists, such as Missy Elliot, did not have any concerts over that time period. Other artists, such as the Red Hot Chili Peppers, performed mostly at mega-festivals thus making their contribution to the total revenue generated very difficult to estimate. And still others, such as Bruno Mars, undertook a world tour where the revenue data was not reported. The result of all this was a data set full of holes. Using the remaining data that was reliable, the results of the sign test did not indicate a statistically significant bump in concert revenues over the time of the study. This is an area ripe for future research. A researcher could further investigate this by focusing solely on concert data, and not linking it to music consumption. This would provide a more robust data set, and lead to perhaps finding different results. At this point, the bump in revenue generated from concerts can only be speculated but not confirmed.

We have evidence that halftime performers do receive substantial benefits from these shows that the NFL is financing. That suggests the NFL is subsidizing these performers. Why might they do that?

Our first approach to this question was a theoretical examination that considered the mercantilist incentives of the NFL. Using a dictator game from game theory, it was shown how the NFL could benefit from charging the artists for the right to perform at the game. However, when a nested game approach was used, it was shown that the NFL could harm itself by charging the artists. The presence of fans, who influence the payoffs of the game, could detract from the overall gains seen by the league. In other words, the costs of charging the artists would exceed the benefits to the NFL and the league would not pursue this policy. Similarly, a game theoretic explanation of why an artist may choose not to accept the invitation to be the halftime artist was given. Again, using a nested game approach, the artists could have their fan base diminished if performing at an NFL game was seen as being at odds with an issue stance widely held by their fans. It is left to game theorists and future researchers to explore this concept in more depth and to develop a more complete theory about the influence of fans on the payoffs in these types of games.

Beyond the game theoretic approach, though, is the simple idea that we can explain outcomes by looking at the bargaining power of the participants. As we noted, the NFL started presenting an extensive halftime show because a rival network was poaching its halftime audience with better programming. To stop this from happening, the NFL needed to employ stars capable of having a wide enough appeal to make certain the audience wouldn't leave when the game wasn't being played. The supply of such stars is rather small, hence putting the NFL at a disadvantaged in negotiations.

As a consequence, stars can essentially earn a substantial reward for a show the NFL pays to make happen. Consider the most recent halftime show. In 2020, the halftime show featured Jennifer Lopez and Shakira. Following their show, video and audio streaming of their music increased by 193% to 31.1 million streams from the previous day (Caulfield 2020a). Their music sales also increased by 893% on the day of the game (Caufield 2020b). Their halftime show also generated over 1,300 complaints to the Federal Communications Commission with concerns about inappropriate dancing (Flores 2020) although much of what they did was similar to many performances by the NFL's cheerleaders.

In contrast to Jennifer Lopez and Shakira, though, the cheerleaders are typically not well compensated for their dancing. The most famous cheerleaders—the Dallas Cowboys Cheerleaders—weren't even paid to appear at the 1978 Super Bowl. The Cowboys also reportedly earned more than $1 million on a poster of this cheerleading squad in the 1970s for which the cheerleaders were paid nothing.

Today, the pay of some NFL cheerleaders has improved. The Raiderettes recently won a lawsuit that guarantees those cheerleader would be paid the minimum wage in California. Yes, historically cheerleaders were paid less than minimum wage but today they are paid as well as a new hire at Burger King!

We presented evidence that cheerleaders are worth quite a bit more than just minimum wage. But because they lack bargaining power, the NFL ends up paying these performers far less than their economic value. In essence, cheerleaders are in the same position as professional athletes without free agency rights. They might love their job. But their team is taking advantage of them!

The NFL is the king of sports in the United States and the Super Bowl is the crowning event of the season. The game holds the national interest and generates substantial ratings and revenues. We have seen, though, the game doesn't really benefit too many people associated with the game. The host city and winning team receive far less than what one might imagine. The cheerleaders get far less. As for the stars of the show? The winning quarterback appears to get something. But maybe it is the halftime performer that walks away with the most of all!

References

Caufield, K. (2020a, February 6). Jennifer Lopez & Shakira See Super Streaming Bump After Super Bowl Halftime Show. *Billboard*. Retrieved from https://www.billboard.com/articles/news/super-bowl/8550364/jennifer-lopez-shakira-streaming-bump-super-bowl-halftime-show.

Caufield, K. (2020b, February 4). Jennifer Lopez & Shakira's Song Catalog Nets 893% Sales Gain After Super Bowl. *Billboard*. Retrieved from https://www.billboard.com/articles/business/chart-beat/8550061/jennifer-lopez-shakira-song-catalog-huge-super-bowl-sales-gain.

Flores, G. (2020, February 27). Jennifer Lopez & Shakira Super Bowl Halftime Show Draws More Than 1,000 FCC Complaints. *Billboard*. Retrieved from https://www.billboard.com/articles/columns/latin/9324535/jennifer-lopez-shakira-super-bowl-halftime-show-draws-more-than-1000-fcc-complaints.

Scully, G. (1974). Pay and Performance in Major League Baseball. *American Economic Review, 64*, 915–930.

Index

Y. J. Kelly et al., *The Economics of the Super Bowl*, Palgrave Pivots in Sports Economics, https://doi.org/10.1007/978-3-030-46370-0

The manufacturer's authorised representative in the EU is Springer Nature Customer Service Centre GmbH, Europaplatz 3, 69115 Heidelberg, Germany. If you have any concerns regarding our products, please contact ProductSafety@springernature.com

Printed and bound by CPI Group (UK) Ltd, Croydon, CR0 4YY
30/09/2026
02225475-0014